1979

Environmental Planning for Children's Play

Environmental Planning for Children's Play

by ARVID BENGTSSON

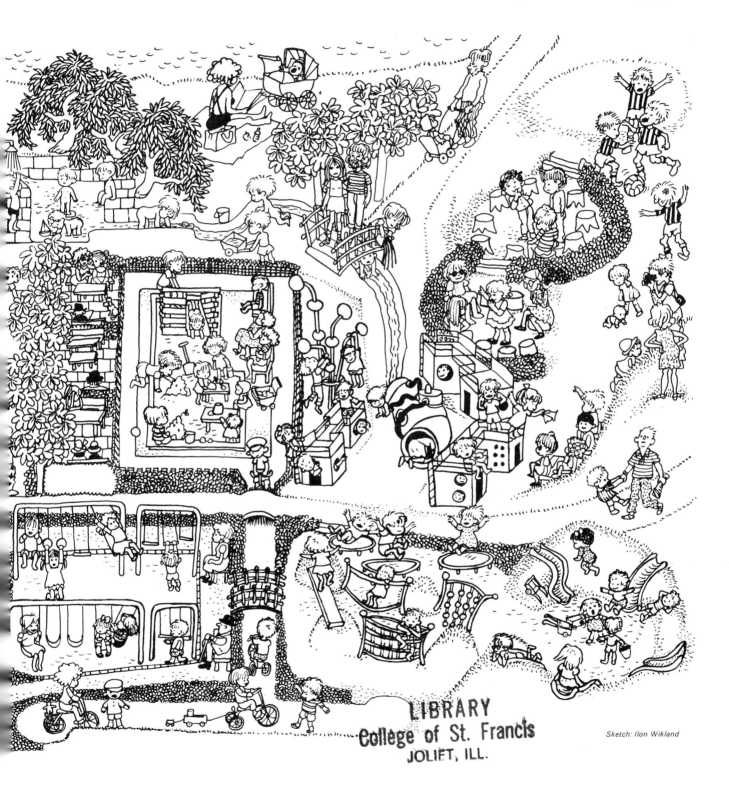

Sketch: Ilon Wikland

PRAEGER PUBLISHERS New York · Washington

BOOKS THAT MATTER

Published in the United States of America in 1970
by Praeger Publishers, Inc.
111 Fourth Avenue, New York, N.Y. 10003

© 1970 in London, England by Arvid Bengtsson

Library of Congress Catalog Card Number: 79–112771

Printed in Great Britain

Contents

711.558
B468

86700

INTRODUCTION

"The time has come to focus attention on this extremely important problem which confronts the children and youth of to-day, particularly in heavily built-up areas where young people are subject to the dangers of the street". These words of Maurice Milhaud, Chief of the United Nations' Technical Assistance Administration, initiated the report of the European Seminar on the problem of playgrounds, held in 1958 by the United Nations at Bergendal outside Stockholm. From that moment the matter progressed from being a town-gardener's special concern into a social question of such importance that the world organisation considered it essential to work towards a means to its solution.

Increasingly, motor traffic has impeded the orderly development of our towns, and as a result play areas for children have become dangerously limited. Our modern residential districts are certainly greener than before; the old slum backyards have been replaced by flowering gardens and the dark narrow streets have been cleared, bringing the sun to indoor and out-door spaces. But the excitement of the backyard as a playground has disappeared and the sandpit in the new courtyard does not make up for the loss. With ever-increasing motor traffic the street has ceased to be a playground, although it still attracts children in spite of its dangers. Efficient planning has led to the disappearance of derelict plots of land and has improved welfare and hygiene but in so doing it has removed a great deal of traditional play material. Even the adult world, a major source of inspiration for children's games, no longer centres on the home, and the result is the dormitory town most of us know only too well. The children's playworld has been the loser in all these respects.

We must not forget that the old town was, generally speaking, a town of pedestrians where children and adults moved virtually unobstructed by wheeled traffic. In such towns the planned playground —insofar as it existed—was a luxury since it was not really essential. It was a pleasure ground in miniature which one could either afford or do without, depending on cost and convenience. It is disturbing that most of the playgrounds now being planned and built at great expense all over the world still follow the nineteenth century pattern, in spite of the radical revolution that society has undergone. Added to this, today's children have perhaps more time for play than ever before, since they begin their working lives much later and only occasionally assist in their parents' occupation.

Something just had to happen! It amounted to nothing less than a demand for human rights for that section of the population which lacks voice and representation in our councils and governments, and is entirely dependent on our care. The growth of juvenile crime is one of many signs that not all is as it should be. The aggressive confrontation of the generations is another. Not everything can be blamed on the lack of facilities for play, but it is clearly a supplementary reason. We *do* more for the coming generation than ever before, but our "doing" is more concerned with guiding them towards a safe income than giving them a full and worthwhile life. The fun and joy of living, which should last us through life, all too often dies in childhood.

Awareness of the problems peculiar to urban environment is now increasing and the debate is often heated and highly critical of solutions found so far. Most certainly it will itensify. There will be no lack of argument, but what has been missing is a positive programme, some clear path to follow. This book shows how the problems are being tackled, and if it is something of a "picture book" this is because the presentation of actual schemes from all over the world is more effectively done with photographs and drawings than long descriptive text.

It does not offer any outright solution. We have by no means heard the final word on creating the ideal play-society, and among that that has been done there is little that could not be improved upon.

SOME VIEWS ON THE MICROCLIMATE

Neither plants nor animals thrive in a draught, and it is surprising that this factor is so often ignored in our outdoor environment. Many residental areas are exposed to winds from all directions and it seems to be assumed that such winds are a phenomenon as difficult to control as rain and snow. Fortunately this is not the case. Every gardener knows the importance to plants of shelter from the wind and how to protect them. Fishing communities along our coasts have, since olden times, built close housing villages and towns for the sake of shelter, and the old enclosed courtyard-type farms on the plains are another example. Shelter from wind is still one of the most important conditions for comfort out of doors.

In this context wind shelter is a question of correct planning. The low, dense town gives a better microclimate than the tall, open town, and it is evident that low rise housing is more serviceable as protection against wind than the point block. Walls and hoardings, hedges, rows of trees, garages and other small buildings are further examples of the useful fixtures available. The large volume of surplus material from building sites, which is often disposed of at great expense, could advantageously be used for creating shelter. In several cases this has been done with great success. The rampart has a long history and has served various purposes, not all of them military. It gives excellent protection against noise and wind, and can be of pleasant architectural value. In the case of old military layouts there are many opportunities for the study of architectural method and effect. A rampart built as a wind break should, unlike the military version, be planted with trees and bushes, for it is well known that a screen of vegetation to filter the wind is a far more effective shelter than a screen which is close and unyielding.

Vegetation, once established, is therefore a very efficient weapon in the battle against winds. Some well placed screens can work wonders if the buildings are not too large and the air currents not too strong. Shelter against wind is also, in part, shelter against cold.

A person who lives in northern Europe and spends much of the year longing for sun and warmth may find it almost blasphemous to talk about shelter from the sun, but even in the north the need must be considered, especially insofar as playgrounds are concerned. Children and parents often have quite different views on the merits of the sun. Parents want suntanned children, but children may prefer to spend a summer day in the shade, even though the heat may not bother the adults. Children are, of course, especially sensitive to strong sunlight, and it is important that shady play areas should be available. As far as cold shade during the winter months is concerned, both children and parents agree—it is unpleasant for everybody. In a northern climate the main part of a playground should be sunny, with shady areas for use when needed and the entrance on a sunny side.

A matter which deserves special consideration is that of shadows cast by buildings themselves, which often have a ruinous effect on the immediate surroundings. For instance, a ten-storey "slab" block, however placed, has a most inconvenient shadow. If placed on an east-west axis its northern side will be cold and unpleasant and will be useless for the greater part of the year, except, possibly, as a car park. If the building is placed on a north-south axis each side will be in deep shade for half of the day. In such cases it is most desirable to have entrance halls linking both sides so that the children can readily choose the side on which to play.

Large buildings influence their surroundings in many ways. The larger the building the greater the air mass influenced and the stronger the forces created. There are housing areas where there is always a gale blowing, even if the wind outside the area is comparatively light.

These are some ways in which the microclimate can be influenced. A little interference can have drastic results, for the better and for the worse. It is most unfortunate that, until recently, the creation of satisfactory conditions out of doors has been left more or less to chance.

Neither plants nor humans thrive in a draught and it is surprising that this factor is so often ignored in our outdoor environment.

Elburg, Holland

The low, dense town gives a better
microclimate than the tall, open town,
and it is evident that low-rise housing
is more serviceable as protection
against wind than the point block.

11

Sketch: Cecilia Bengtsson

OUTDOORS—INDOORS

In the ideal dwelling for a family with children a boundary between outdoors and indoors hardly exists. The child moves freely from one to the other, enlarging the radius of its activities as its feelings of safety and self-reliance grow. As it investigates, the outside world increases the child's own experience. The escape route back to the mother, or her substitute, is always there, and this greatly strengthens the child's self-confidence. In the ideal world there is no sudden plunge into the unknown.

Unfortunately the day-to-day reality rarely lives up to this ideal. It requires courage for a small person to risk the descent from a flat in a tall block to ground level, with all its real and imagined dangers; not to mention the courage—or even rashness—that the mother must possess before sending him down there. This courage is often lacking on both sides, and the child stays indoors, except when child and parent go out together.

To many children living in tall blocks, ground level remains a foreign world for years and they feel lonely and isolated as a result. A recent investigation in London showed that of children under 5 years of age, living above fourth floor level in the examined area, 72% seldom played with other children of their own age. Investigations in Czechoslovakia (Juri Musil 1964) have shown similar results.

In 1960 a comparative investigation was carried out in Stockholm (Wohlin) of 3–4 storey and 8–13 storey apartment blocks. The survey showed that children in the lower blocks were out of doors for about one hour longer per day than those in the other group, and that they went in and out of the block twice as many times, often on their own or with a playmate. In the taller blocks the children were usually accompanied by the mother or another adult.

The conclusion from all such investigations is the same. Living in a tall block has grave consequences for the family, and we must not shut our eyes to this. If high rise development is continued it will be necessary to accept the implications and arrange communal child supervision in an appropriate manner because this can, to a certain degree, help overcome the problem of contact between children. Lack of contact is a serious matter and can be the cause of neuroses, with unfortunate effects on the development of the personality.

To quote the United States National Education Association : "Research shows clearly that the first four or five years of a child's life is the period of most rapid growth in physical and mental characteristics and of greatest susceptibility to environment influence. Consequently, it is in the early years that deprivation is most disastrous in its effect."

In the ideal dwelling the child moves freely from indoors to outdoors, enlarging the radius of activity as its feelings of safety and self-reliance grow.

To many children ground level remains a foreign world for years and they feel lonely and isolated as a result.

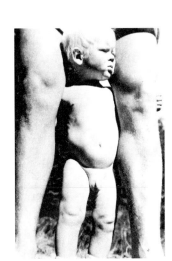

1

1 A close town community in contrast with
   the surrounding countryside. Chambéry
   Croix Rouge, France
2 A lunch break nap in the park
3 Down town

A DIFFERENTIATED OUTDOOR ENVIRONMENT

2

A great drawback to many new town areas is that they offer only two kinds of outdoor environment: a traffic- and a sandpit-environment, the latter sometimes replaced by an ornamental space for visual enjoyment only. As a result, children beyond the sandpit age are usually very badly off for outdoor facilities, and conditions for adults are seldom much better. Even so, one can hardly complain that our newer towns are lacking in open spaces! Compared with older town developments they are often generously provided. What is usually lacking is concentration. Buildings and open spaces are too often evenly mixed like the ingredients in a salad with the result that contrasts are levelled and all elements become more or less equally large—or equally small.
What I should like to see is a close and intimate town community, and, to contrast with this, parks and other open spaces for varying purposes, each laid out in accordance with its proper function in the composition of the town, and located according to today's knowledge of acceptable walking distance and "catchment" areas.

Keep off the grass
The sign is not popular, but it should be remembered that the best way to abolish it is at the town planning stage. Afterwards, the sign, and its observance, may be the only way to ensure the survival of an undersized lawn. A logical solution would be to use hard surfaces which we know will last, but with our unconcentrated way of building towns, and the large areas thus involved, it is an expensive alternative, one which also might be quite disastrous to the environment itself if not done with great ingenuity.

On the other hand, with a dense urban development it is often natural to choose hard-wearing surfaces which emphasise the urban character. Concentration has the additional advantage of freeing resources which may be used for parks large enough to stand the wear without prohibitions or fences. This would bring not only practical and

3

economical advantages but also a richer and more varied town community.

We need different kinds of urban spaces
Too little is said and written about town spaces and, to judge from many recent developments, they do not receive much consideration from town planners either. The result can be chaos, bitter draughts and general discomfort. As housing producers we seem over-absorbed in the problem of interiors. The spaces between the buildings are too often haphazardly formed, even though they are vital to the overall result. The outdoor environment needs no less consideration than the interior, and it is important that both are considered together.

We need outdoor spaces of different kinds and dimensions to satisfy the various age groups and their various needs. We need small and intimate spaces in the immediate proximity of the dwellings (which is where small children spend most of their outdoor life), but we also need larger areas, not too far away, for the more space-demanding and noisy activities. We need rooms for rest and relaxation and, perhaps, decorative areas to take a pride in, just as we certainly need spaces to use as freely as we wish, without worrying about how untidy or messy they may look.

5

4

6

4, 5, 6, 7, 8   There should be room for every-body and a great variety of alternatives to choose from

7

18

8

PLAY TRAFFIC—MOTOR TRAFFIC

Investigations in Stockholm (Wohlin, Sandels) have confirmed what we have known by long experience, that children play wherever they happen to be at that moment, unaffected by what architects and builders had in mind, and irrespective of whether the area is "suitable" or not. The focal point of their outdoor existence seems to be the entrance to the house. If it faces a car park or the street, they will play dangerously amongst the traffic or parked cars. If it faces a planned playground, they will play there. But in the first case this does not mean that, because of the risks involved, they should not play ! Far from it.

2

1

Children love to run risks, love to be right in the centre of the events. A parking area has its advantages as a playground. Its cars become a labyrinth where anything can happen behind the next vehicle and, what is more, it usually has a smooth surface, which is just right for riding bicycles and driving toy cars. Children play happily in streets and in car parks, but we must do our utmost to keep them away from these dangerous playgrounds. But how ? *Surely it*

cannot be done just by laying out playgrounds, however well arranged and however valuable we consider them to be. The problem is much more complicated.

The play community of the street
City children have always played outside their homes in their own street, and still do. The street has been the uniting factor, giving a sense of belonging and security against other children of other streets. The children of each street formed a community against the outside world even if,

amongst themselves, their solidarity could at times be rather doubtful. In principle the street has changed very little in that respect, in spite of the metamorphosis it has undergone with regard to traffic.

Segregation of traffic
If in our planning of new developments we want to move children away from the traffic of the streets to safer playgrounds, we must be prepared to move the complete play-community. Either we move traffic and street parking and let the

1, 2, 3   Children play wherever they happen to be, whether the area is "suitable" or not

3

21

street resume its function of former days, or we create conditions for a new community away from the street. In fact, it is exactly this which has led to the most radical revolution in town planning of this century—traffic segregation. By this we mean a town development where motor traffic is strictly separated from walking and playing traffic. Theoretically, the principle is universally accepted but, unfortunately, practically speaking it is not. There is, as usual, a gap between theory and practice, and in too many cases playing children and cars are still allowed to intermingle as if nothing had been learned. Consciences are possibly soothed by

a pedestrian bridge or tunnel here and there but, as neither children nor adults will walk ten more steps to find a safer route, this measure is quite inadequate, especially if the street still functions as a play community. Traffic segregation is the only solution and lies at the heart of the matter. It can't be added afterwards. The removal of the play community is a thorough operation, which cannot be achieved by half measures. One of the deciding factors in achieving the desired result seems to be the positioning of the entrances to the houses, because the entrance side will always be the play side.

Furthermore the pedestrian road has to be the shortest route, or at least give the impression of being so, otherwise people will take short cuts despite any danger involved.

It is only too easy to assume that traffic safety is a matter for concern in big cities alone, but this is certainly not the case. In fact, it is specifically the small streets with sporadic traffic which claim the most victims among playing children. On main roads the danger is so obvious that everyone pays more attention to it.

Those who oppose traffic segregation often argue that children

4, 5 The way to school is an important play-street, and must be safe
6 A smooth, hard surface for wheels of all sizes
7 Bad planning makes for costly maintenance
8 A variety of surfaces is desirable

4

5

7

6

communication. The layout of the whole neighbourhood must be studied to give an idea of how play traffic is going to move. The way to school is an important route for play, as is the way to the shops. But perhaps the most important of all is the area in front of the apartment block, especially for the smaller children, and it is these places which are usually the first to show wear in a traditionally planned area. All playgrounds have to be suitably linked with this "playstretch" or they will never be of any importance. There are several examples of perfectly good playgrounds almost completely unused because they were unrelated to their surroundings.

We often plan as if play was a kind of task which the child takes to the playground to perform. But the substance of play is something completely different. Tommy may be on his way to school or running an errand for his mother, but he is also the driver of the latest sports car he has just seen around the corner. He is the fastest thing on wheels; he slams the breaks on, the whole of the "vehicle" screeching, then accelerates to top speed, at the same time keeping half an eye on the public's reaction. Tommy is acting a

must get used to traffic and that it is a risk to let them grow up in a traffic-sheltered community. We know, however, through established research (Sandels) that even 11–12 year old children are not equipped to encounter the dangers of traffic. They lack ability to judge a situation, can only take in one thing at a time, and are still imprisoned in their world of play. We know, too, that the frequency of accidents amongst playing children is related to planning. We have town areas with a high frequency of accidents and others with a low one, despite the fact that the density of traffic is the same in each.

Planning for play
We too often forget that planning for play is very much a question of

8

9

part which varies with mood and stimulus. Play is a constant happening, a constant act of creation in the mind or in practice. The smaller the child, the more narrow the circle in which it moves, but even older children spend most of their playing time within a radius of rarely more than 300 m (350 yd) from home. Remember, when planning for play, that playgrounds must be within easy reach.

The "play stretch" should offer a whole series of possibilities. A small slope, which can make a toy car self-mobile, is a positive addition ; a climbing-rock from which to survey the world need not be very large ; some raised stepping-stones give impulses for play, especially if they can be extended to form a small system so that the child can move a long way without touching the ground. A mound of sand has a constructive potential which can provide many hours of occupation. A balancing pole may be a bit difficult for a small child but for that reason may have a special element of attraction.

The choice of surface is important.

Hard smooth surfaces are needed as well as soft ones. We need variety.

Quiet "play-stretches" should be supplemented by more or less active playgrounds depending on circumstances, all of them to some extent serving as meeting places.

This programme might seem ambitious but one must not forget that in the old days—not at all long ago—the "play-stretch" was provided by a network of roads which spread all over town and embraced the adult world with its multitude of workshops and markets of different kinds. A planned "play-stretch", however ambitious, can only be a pale substitute.

10

Are all open spaces meant for children ?

The answer to this question must be "yes" and "no". Children should be admitted to open spaces under the same conditions as adults. To split a town into ghettoes for different age groups is absurd. It is a question of making different areas attractive and suitable for various types of activity, and at the same time trying to retain as much flexibility as possible.

11

12

13

Bad planning costs money
It is fortunate that children do not
stop playing when our planning is a
failure, but we pay for our failures
with high maintenance costs. Each
year we spend enormous sums on
layouts to maintain their upkeep at a
bare minimum, but they are bound to
be worn out because they were not
planned with children's needs and
behaviour in mind. We have been
trying too long to force children's
play into our garden patterns, even
when we know deep inside us that
they will not work. The social aspects
of the outdoor environment certainly
deserve special consideration, but
they are too often neglected. Green,
well-kept grass is pleasing to the eye,
but if a sign "Keep off the grass"
restricts the child's natural play
element, it is time to protest.

14

9, 10, 11 *Children spend most of their playing*
          time close to home
12 *They often commandeer what was not*
    provided voluntarily
13 *Special measures may be needed to keep*
    cars out
14 *Playing just outside the doorway*

Three residential areas in Örebro, Sweden

1 BARONBACKARNA

Architects: B. Alm, P. A. Ekholm, R. Falk, S. White.
Built 1954–57, the area contains about 1,200 flats.

Örebro is a small town of no more than 85,000 inhabitants, but it is a town with ambitions which, in matters of housing and environment, believes that only the best is good enough. In recent years, almost all projected new housing estates have been the subject of town planning competitions, the winner of the first prize being commissioned to plan the projected area. In this way, Örebro secured a leading position in Swedish town planning and has influenced the building of housing estates all over the country. Baronbackarna, Markbacken and Vivalla are three examples of this housing estate policy.

The town plan is constructed on the principle of a logical separation of pedestrian and vehicular traffic. A loop of three- and four-storey developments encircles a central park area and separates the traffic area from the play sector. Traffic, including parking areas and garages, has thus been kept outside the

development, while schools, day nurseries, playgrounds and shops lying within it can be reached from all flats without crossing any roads.

In 1962, the National Swedish Institute for Building Research made a study of the utilization of free areas at Baronbackarna. It found that the traffic differentiation functioned well

1

2

and that very few children ventured outside the boundary formed by the loop of buildings. About 70 per cent of the mothers of two- to four-year-old children interviewed said that their children normally play out of doors unaccompanied by adults. The children play mostly in their own courtyard. This applies primarily to children up to the age of 11; children above that age often spend their time in the park. Few children are seen outside the housing development under the age of 15.

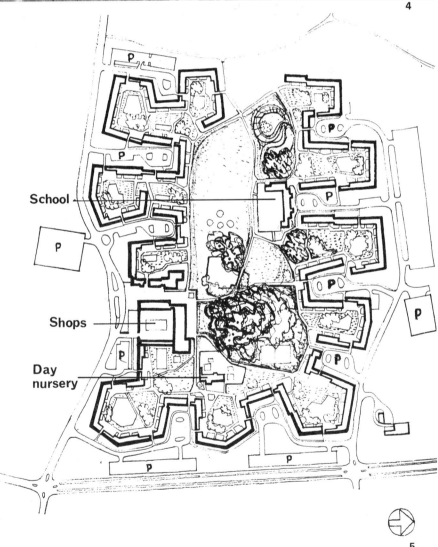

School

Shops

Day nursery

1 The homes enclose the central park area
2 The serenity of the park area in contrast to a traffic environment
3 The original vegetation and contours remain
4 Waterplay in the park
5 Plan of the development

2 MARKBACKEN

Architects: WAAB White AB

The area lies on level ground and has a total of 1,231 flats. Constructed 1959–63.

The larger of the three housing units included in the development has been built with a similar system of traffic differentiation to Baronbackarna; that is, an outer traffic quarter and an inner park quarter where schools and playgrounds are situated, with an adjacent shopping centre. No vehicular traffic is permitted within this area.

All entrances to the flats face the play side. The courtyards have spacious and robust playgrounds near the entrances, and fenced-in gardens whose greenery encloses quiet playgrounds. In this way a certain balance has been secured between vegetation and hard-surfaced areas. In each courtyard there is a detached laundry with large windows which allow mothers to keep an eye on their children in the playground.

The large central grass area is able to withstand heavy wear because of its size and simple form.

Pedestrian and cycle paths connect the various housing units of the area and cross the vehicle streets by flyovers or tunnels.

The smaller housing unit in the western part of the area has a different type of traffic separation to that of the larger unit. The entire traffic environment is sunk in relation to the playstreet and separated from it by a wall. The parking area is reached by stairs. The playstreet system continues between the buildings, the inner courtyard being a quiet garden quarter which provides the ground floor flats with their own outside area undisturbed by children's play.

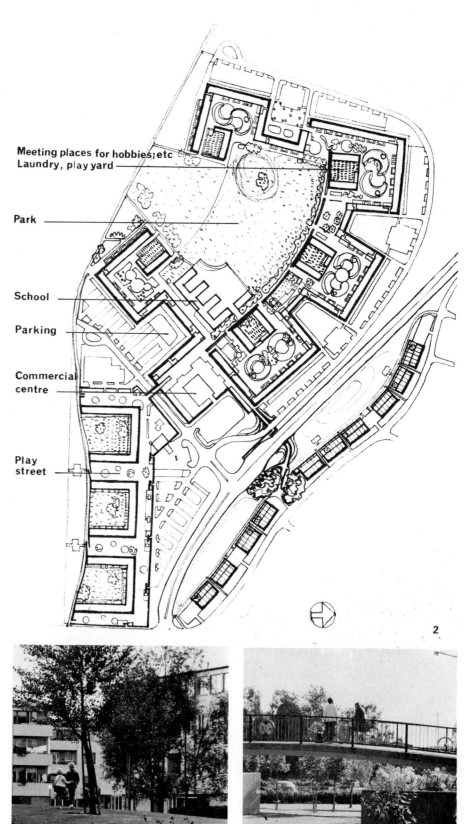

Meeting places for hobbies; etc
Laundry, play yard

Park

School

Parking

Commercial centre

Play street

2

1

3

28

5

1 Coming home from school
2 Plan
3 Pedestrian and cyclist flyover
4 The 'courtyard' is laid out for children's
   play, and not as a garden
5 Traffic segregation is thorough
6 Pedestrian and cyclist underpass
7 Protection against cold winds should be
   provided

6

4

7

3 VIVALLA

Architects: Bertil Hulten, Lennart Kvarnström.
Landscape architects: Sven-Ingvar Andersson, Bruno Richter.

Construction of the Vivalla housing estate began in summer 1967 and is expected to be completed by 1970. The development is wholly two-storey buildings, and its 2,538 flats make it the largest low-building project carried out in Sweden. It is worth noticing that two-storey building, formerly considered uneconomical, has been proved at Vivalla to compare very favourably economically with modern tower block developments.

Vivalla is also a very interesting estate from other points of view, especially that of the child, who is literally right at the centre of things. The development is, consequently, grouped around playgrounds. The smallest unit consists of the "courtyard" situated between the buildings. This is enclosed by fencing to an outer "room", well integrated with the surroundings and in direct contact with the residences. The courtyard is the playground for the small children, and has been designed with their play needs in mind.

All the courtyards are in direct contact with *the playground for the somewhat older children*, which forms the core in a group of buildings of about 250 flats. This playground has the character of a park, and acts as the communal meeting point within the group of buildings; at the same time it is in direct, vehicle-free, contact with the central play park, with schools and shopping centre. Apart from play arrangements, it also contains a collective laundry for the group, as well as club premises and a nursery (day nursery and afternoon nursery for school children whose parents work away from the home).

The play park consists mainly of a large grass playing field surrounded by a dense growth of trees.

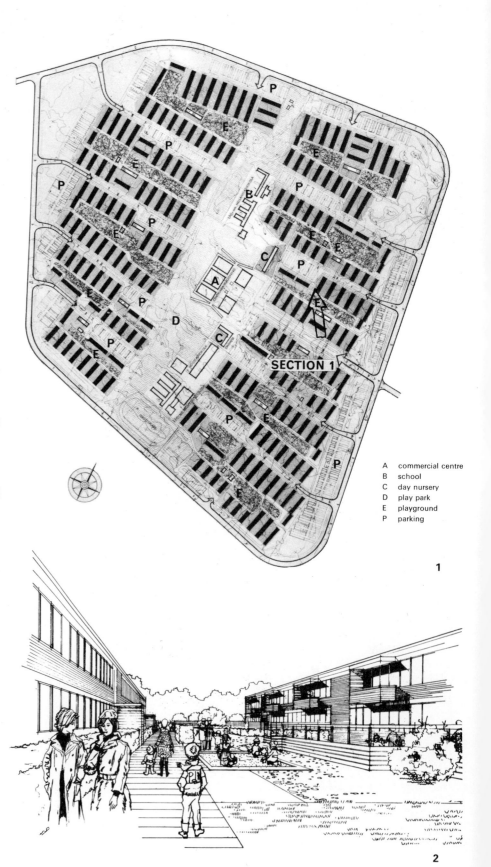

A commercial centre
B school
C day nursery
D play park
E playground
P parking

1

2

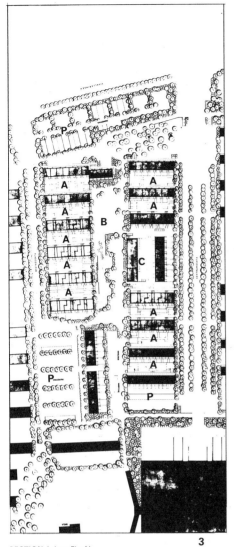

SECTION 1 (see Fig 1)
A   play yard
B   playground
C   day nursery,
    after school home
P   parking

3

5

6

1   Site plan
2   Play yard between the houses
3   Group of enclosed play yards (Section 1)
    around a common play area
4   The houses with their enclosed play yards
    seen from the playground
5   Play yard between the houses
6   Sketch of the play area
7   Layout of the play yard area

4

7

A   sand box
B   simple equipment
C   private garden
D   wooden wall

Albertslund, Denmark

Architect: Knud Svensson.
Landscape Architect: Ole Nørgård.

Albertslund is a new town about 15 km (9 miles) west of Copenhagen. When fully developed it will have 30,000—40,000 inhabitants. In the section shown here there are about 7,000.

As far as traffic is concerned the area fails to provide the segregation which we have every reason to expect nowadays. The car penetrates deeply into the finely meshed traffic network and the central thoroughfare is long and straight, inviting fast driving.

In spite of this defect, however,

Albertslund is one of the most interesting townplanning projects of recent years. It is a garden town in many respects, with an urban character which has but little in common with its British ancestors. To try to judge Albertslund from the available pictorial evidence is asking a lot of the reader, since the size of the freshly planted trees bear no relation to the important part they will play in the town structure in a few years time. The greenery in Albertslund is such an integral part of the layout that it cannot be excluded without the most serious consequences.

1

2

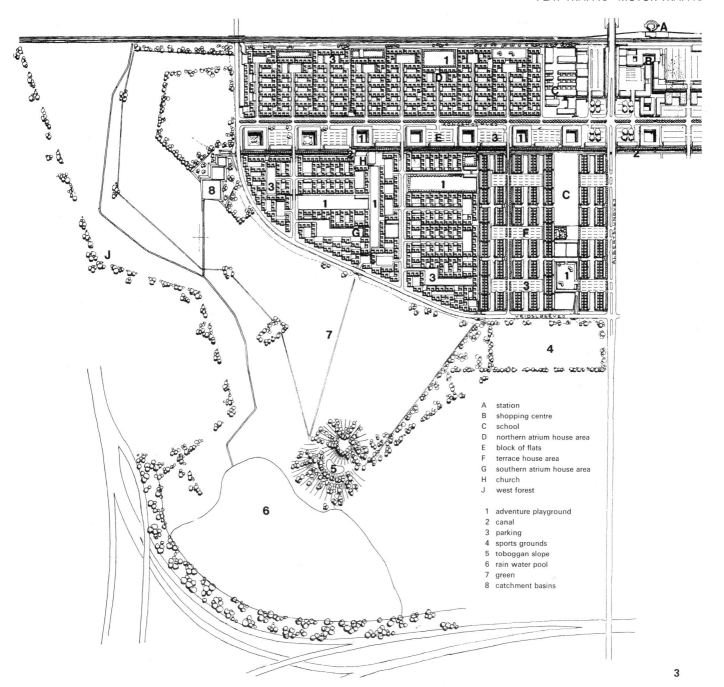

A station
B shopping centre
C school
D northern atrium house area
E block of flats
F terrace house area
G southern atrium house area
H church
J west forest

1 adventure playground
2 canal
3 parking
4 sports grounds
5 toboggan slope
6 rain water pool
7 green
8 catchment basins

3

Albertslund has a very definite cellular composition, all parts of which—even the outdoor spaces—have their special functions. Streets, paths, squares, gardens and courtyards, buildings, etc. are consistently of a scale which shows that human beings were the working module.

Albertslund is an alternative to high housing as we usually know it, where contact between indoor and outdoor life is often entirely lacking, and where conditions of space out of doors are often chaotic, to say the least. It is an interesting alternative well worthy of attention.

1 Narrow lane between the atrium houses
2 Play street in the area of terraced houses
3 Plan
4 Hill for tobogganing

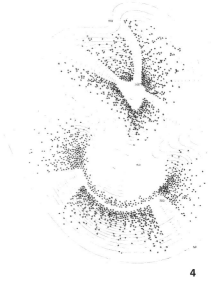

4

6

7

5

5 Playground and meeting place
6 Adventure playground
7, 9, 11 Play streets
8 Courtyard
10 Canal

10

8

11

9

Brittgården, Tibro, Sweden

Architect: Ralph Erskine, ARIBA.

The housing development at Brittgården on the outskirts of Tibro is comparatively small—311 flats in multi-family houses and 57 single-family houses. For a small community like Tibro (6,500 inhabitants) it is, however, quite a large unit, of original and independent character.

The project provides for a large inter-connected car-free sector within a short distance of the streets and parking. The three-storey houses, facing north, east and west, form a town wall surrounding an inner area of terraced houses and atrium houses making a safe, sheltered play environment.

The landscaping has been done in such a way that all open space can be used for play. Smooth asphalt surfaces alternate with cobbled surfaces and large blocks of natural stone. The greenery within the housing area itself consists mainly of trees and bushes. The aim has been to create an urban character in pleasant contrast to the adjoining park.

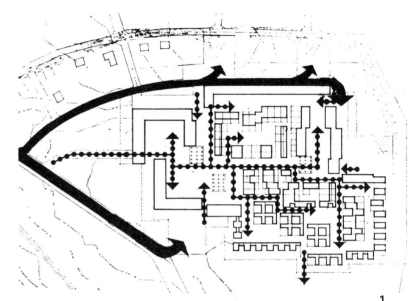

1

2

4

3

5

1   Site plan showing segregation of traffic
2, 3, 4   The whole traffic-free area is available
     for play
5   Model of the development

7

6

8

9

10

6, 7, 10   *Smooth asphalt surfaces alternate*
            with cobbled surfaces and large blocks of
            natural stone
8   *Playing shop in a doorway*
9   *A railing with high play potential*

Residential Estate in Kiruna, Sweden

Architect: Ralph Erskine, ARIBA.

This housing estate was built between 1959 and 1965 on a gentle south-facing slope in the mining town of Kiruna, about 100 miles north of the Arctic Circle. There is a wonderful view over Kebnekaise and the surrounding mountain panorama.

The climatic conditions differ considerably from those usually encountered by the housing developer. The winter is long, cold and dark, with a day that, for weeks, is scarcely more than a short dusk. The summer is brief, but all the more intensive, with the sun sometimes shining round the clock.

Ralph Erskine's housing estate is terraced, with houses of well-balanced height looking towards the sun and the beautiful view. Parking spaces have been provided underground, and the play areas are mainly on the decking. In spite of this, it has been possible to create a rich and varied play environment which has very little in common with the usual prim roof gardens. The whole area has almost the character of a large play sculpture, and the child moves on various levels among large natural blocks of stone, square concrete chimneys, masonry, ramps, steps, etc. In the middle of this there are sunny, wind-sheltered balconies for play and pleasant get-togethers.

2

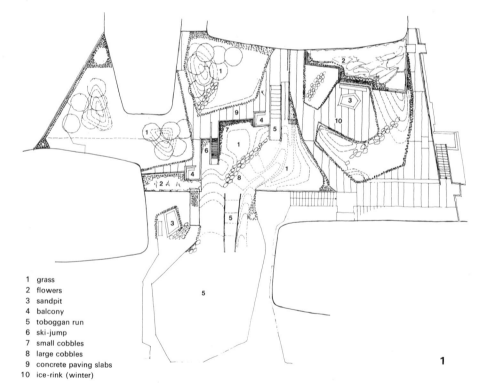

1 grass
2 flowers
3 sandpit
4 balcony
5 toboggan run
6 ski-jump
7 small cobbles
8 large cobbles
9 concrete paving slabs
10 ice-rink (winter)

1

1 Plan of the decked area
2, 3 Play environment
4 Site plan

3

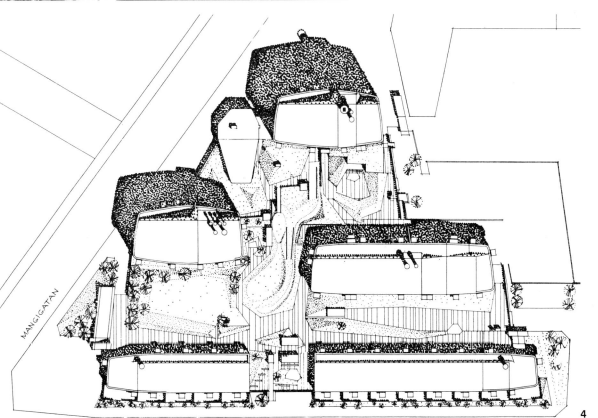

4

Stenby-Löppinge, Eskilstuna, Sweden

Architects: P. A. Ekholm and Per Lundberg.
Landscape architects:
Carl-Vilhelm/Sundin AB

This town planning project is an adaptation of the winning submission in an architectural competition in 1967.

The development is grouped towards the west and east around the Stenby meadow which, in view of its important vegetation and beauty, has been proposed as a park and recreation area.

The planned area comprises 2,760 normal flats. These are divided into 720 flats in six-storey blocks, 420 in three-storey blocks and 1,620 in two-storey blocks. The population is expected to reach 8,200.

The development is arranged in building groups of about 200 flats. Apart from the access road, each group also has common facilities for parking, play, laundry, and bicycle storage.

The traffic differentiation is carried out uniformly. Each building group has direct, vehicle-free, pedestrian access to shops, schools and recreation area. The development to the west of the central supply section is connected by pedestrian subways to that of the east.

The area will be built in stages over a five-year period, commencing 1969–70.

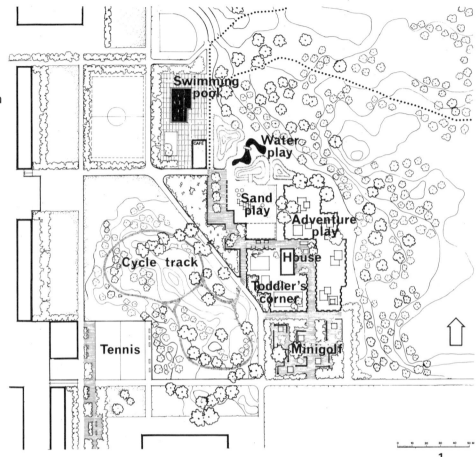

1   Play park
2   Main street (*pedestrian*)
3   Layout of the development

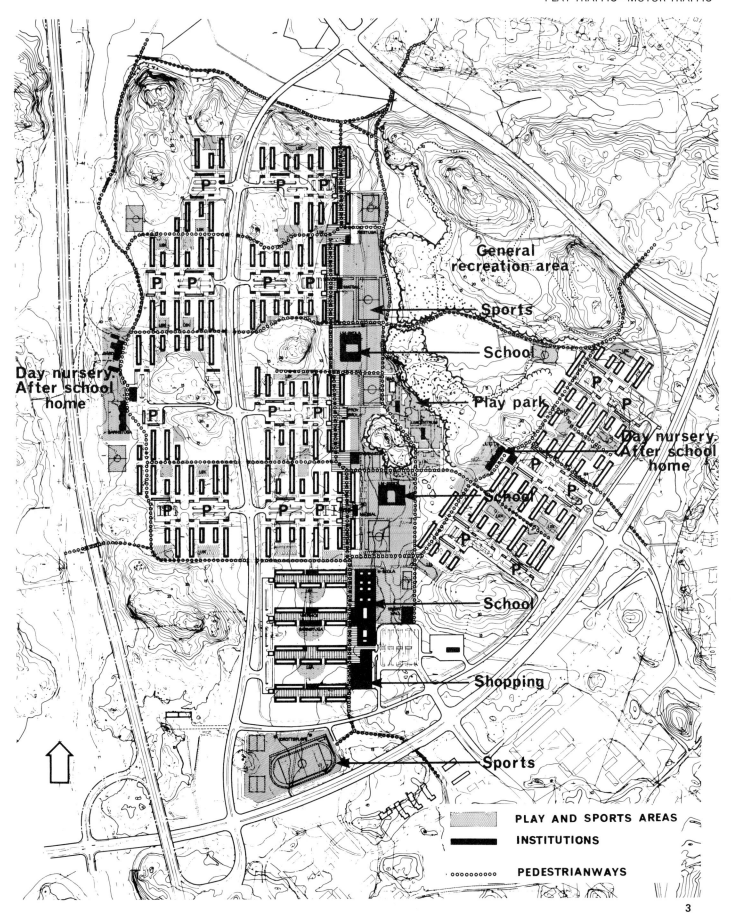

General recreation area

Sports

School

Play park

Day nursery
After school
home

Day nursery
After school
home

School

School

Shopping

Sports

PLAY AND SPORTS AREAS

INSTITUTIONS

ooooooooooo PEDESTRIANWAYS

3

Spaden, North Tynnered, Gothenburg, Sweden

Architects: Per-Axel Ekholm, Per Lundberg.
Landscape architects: Carl-Vilhelm/Sundin.

Spaden is a housing estate that, in my opinion, is very near to the ideal as far as children's play is concerned. Contact between the external and internal is good. The buildings have only three storeys, and all entrances face a common, vehicle-free, street-like area, as in the old days. Each pair of buildings has been provided with its own sandpit, which can easily be supervised from the buildings, and within a few years a line of trees will offer a pleasant interchange between sun and shade. The system of streets makes it possible to walk between the houses

1

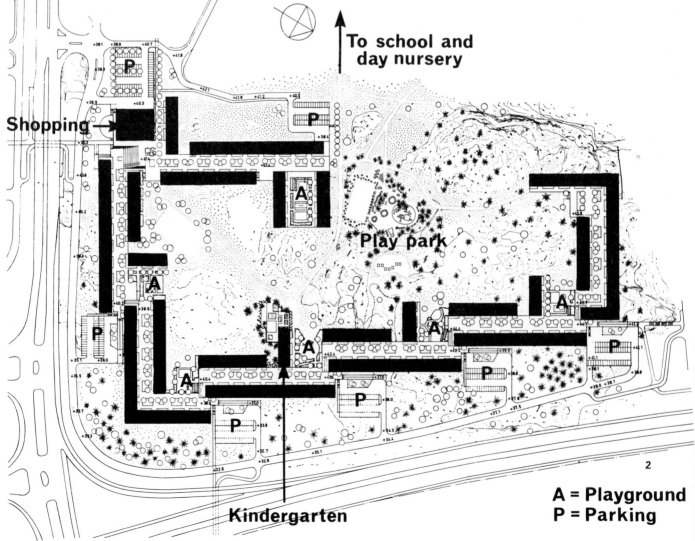

To school and day nursery

Shopping →

Play park

Kindergarten

2

A = Playground
P = Parking

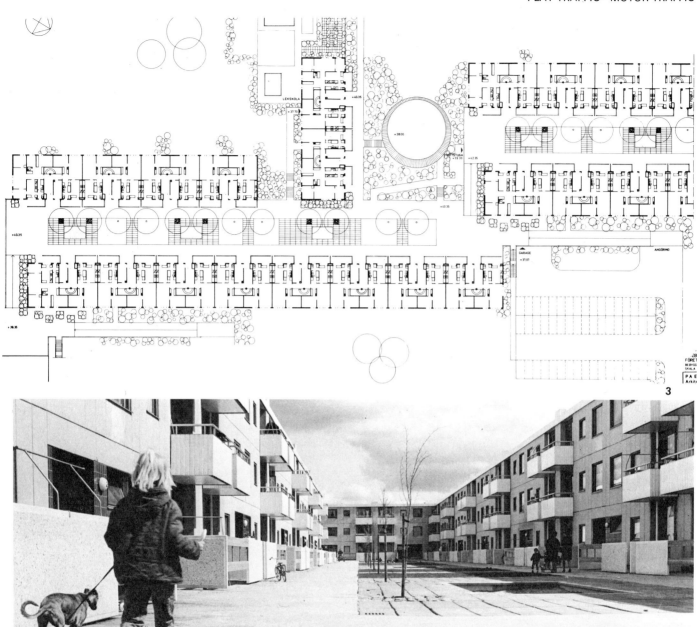

3

4

and to encounter alternately narrow streets and open spaces in strong contrast to the hilly, wooded area forming the play park around which the whole housing estate is grouped. The pedestrian streets have connections to vehicle-free paths which lead to schools, shopping centre and bus stops.

The area consists of 874 flats. The estate has been organised in units of about 110 flats with a common playground, laundry and visitors' parking place. Other parking is mainly provided in garages under the pedestrian streets.

1   The central grass area
2, 3   Plans of estate and playground locality
4   Play street, which has to be imagined with
      grown trees
5   Playground

5

REDEVELOPMENTS

The economic backgrounds of new housing estates built on virgin ground, and the redevelopment of older housing areas, must differ considerably; but as concerns planning for play they follow largely the same rules. Even within the redevelopment areas, the problem is concerned with children whose need is to play as children have always played. What I have said earlier about play planning therefore also applies here, and the requirements as to traffic safety are at least as important. It is not sufficient to provide an old town layout with a new set of buildings, since the old town plan ceased to function under the intrusion of motor traffic. Traffic and car parking must be tackled in such a manner that an area can recapture something of the quiet and sheltered living environment it once enjoyed.

Small children soon become big children

A frequent shortcoming of current redevelopment is that while comparatively generous planning is made for small children little is done for the somewhat older ones. This is a fairly common fault in new housing developments, but it is particularly remarkable in connection with redevelopment. We ask ourselves anxiously what happens when the small child outgrows the sandpit?

Indeed, we already know from experience, but it is rare for this failure to be followed up or reported.

The street used to offer a solution when the backyard became too small and the child felt the urge to get out of sight of parents. The street was part of the world at large and was a wonderful playground in many ways, and it is obvious that somehow we must replace what has been lost. It certainly will not be done simply by providing play equipment. The high cost of land is one obvious difficulty, particularly in the case of the play park, but it is an obstacle that must be overcome one way or another.

Katarina, Stockholm

Slum-clearance investigation carried out by the architects SAR Hans Fog and Bernt Sahlin at the request of the Building Committee of Stockholm.

The present position
The population density and exploitation of available space are high. The total area of approx. 40 hectares (100 acres) had a population of 20,000 in 1960; this includes an important industrial area where about 5,600 are employed. The blocks are small with narrow courtyards. The buildings are of various periods, some as recent as 1940. The through-traffic is fast in all directions, and in certain areas there is hardly anywhere to play out-of-doors.

Suggestions for immediate adoption
The following measures are recommended: in order to go some way towards improving the district all unauthorized through-traffic to be diverted from the area, and only local and business traffic to be allowed; the streets to be planted with trees and the street lighting to be increased; the backyards to be redesigned and planted with vegetation; the maintenance of properties is also to be improved.

Successive renovations
Following an examination of the conditions of age and hygiene of the buildings the district has been divided into four separate groups.

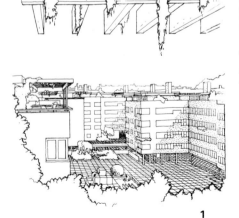

1

2

Three of these contain the older and poorly equipped buildings, of which the first group is to be renovated over a period of ten years and the remainder over subsequent periods of ten years each. The newer and relatively well-equipped buildings make up the fourth group.

Based on this estimated rate of renovation a plan has been drawn up showing a suitable way for its achievement. During the many decisions and compromises of an economic and technical nature which such a complex problem engendered, much thought was given to the provision of places for children to play. An ideal situation regarding play conditions cannot be achieved within the framework of the high exploitation of space granted by town plans still in force, but the changing of the existing diagonal road into a play stretch is certainly a great improvement. As a result of subjecting this stretch, and the adjoining sites and courts, to co-ordinated planning a large central play area has been created to which even the schools are connected.

The traffic segregation is not ideal, but at least a car-free system of communication has been established. As through traffic has been diverted from the district, and car parks are for the most part underground, traffic is slower and safer, and, at the same time, easier to overlook.

3

6

4

1, 3, 4, 5 Final stage
2 Situation of the area in the town of Stockholm
6 Plan of present situation

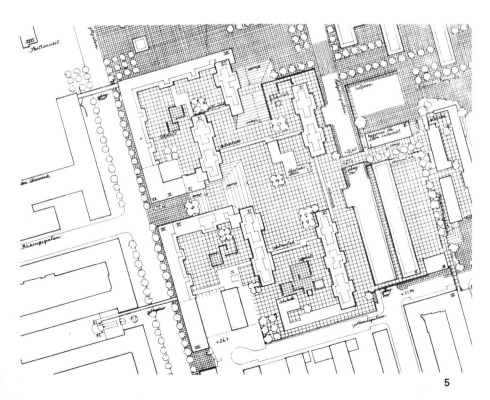

5

D

The old becomes new

Landscape architect: Vera Norin.

The Familjebostäder municipal estate company at Gothenburg has for some years been engaged in a type of redevelopment which, oddly enough, seems unusual today : a renovation of the old slum area in certain central parts of the town. The company buys up all property within the area, renovates it thoroughly and provides it with acceptable sanitary arrangements. The old tenants remain, happy with the improvements but perhaps most happy because they were not required to leave the old well-known part of town.

   The old courtyards, previously divided into small sections by railings, walls or wooden fences, and full of dustbins and outside toilets, are cleaned up and reconstructed with a communal courtyard layout offering good play facilities for small children and a peaceful atmosphere, which also suits the older generation.

2

1

The result is striking : one suddenly discovers that old town environments have qualities lacking in most of the new-qualities which more than compensate, perhaps, for any lack of sunhours in certain flats. Indeed, it could be argued that we pay far too high a price, in our modern housing developments, for these sun-hours at the expense of environment.

The enclosed courtyards of the old renovated estates give a warm and sheltered atmosphere, and the confined space happily stops all ambition towards the planning of grassy areas and their "keep off" signs. Trees and bushes give a garden atmosphere, while almost the whole ground area is freely accessible for play.

3

1, 2   *As it was*
3   *Renovation completed*

Winstanley Road, London

Architects: George, Trew, Dunn.
Landscape architect: Michael Brown.

The site is in a thoroughly run-down area of Battersea which consisted originally of two-storey terraced houses and was entirely lacking in any environmental quality.

In this context the development is interesting above all for the outstanding qualities of landscape design. Great care has been taken to integrate pedestrian movement and circulation with the need for both quiet and more active areas, offering varying degrees of enclosure. Where possible, changes of level have been used to assist in providing "eddies" off the main circulation routes for sitting and for play areas.

A number of different types of playgrounds have been provided around the scheme, but these are less notable than the fact that all outside spaces have been considered potential play spaces. It was felt that children quickly become bored with statically equipped playgrounds, and that their need to climb and run, and feel a sense of enclosure, can just as often be met by walls and benches, by steps and ramps as by equipment which is designed specifically for

1

them. The provision of the right setting, so that children's play may become part of the total environment, has been a primary objective.

The townscape consists predominantly of buildings, hard paving and of trees. The grass areas are small and raised above the adjacent levels, so that for this and other reasons the temptation to "short cut" is slight.

2

1, 3, 4   Pedestrians and playing children
          circulate freely
2   Cars are parked at 'basement' level

3

4

5

6

7

*5, 6, 7   Changes of level have been used
freely*

Stigberget, Gothenburg

Architects: Svenska Riksbyggen
Architects' Office, under the
direction of Hans-Olov Johanson
and Gunnar Serneblad.
Landscape architects:
Carl-Vilhelm Sundin AB.

The redevelopment area is centrally
situated in Gothenburg and lies on
steeply sloping ground which rises
about 45 m (150 feet). The original
development consisted entirely of
wooden houses in a relatively
charming environment, very much
conditioned by the adjacent harbour.
The sanitary standards were low,
however, and playing opportunities
for children were very limited as
vehicles dominated the steep streets
which had once been the children's
playgrounds. A radical redevelopment was therefore considered to be
the solution. It was commenced in
1964 and is planned to be completed
in 1970.

This redevelopment project is
interesting because of the care taken
in creating a good play environment
protected from traffic. All vehicle
traffic, with the exception of
ambulances and fire engines, will be
prohibited within the area, and all
parking will be below ground level.
It will therefore be possible to move
peacefully to shops, schools,
playgrounds, recreation areas and
stopping points for public transport,
and to have vehicle-free contact with
the hilly area at Masthugg Church
and with Slottsskogs park.

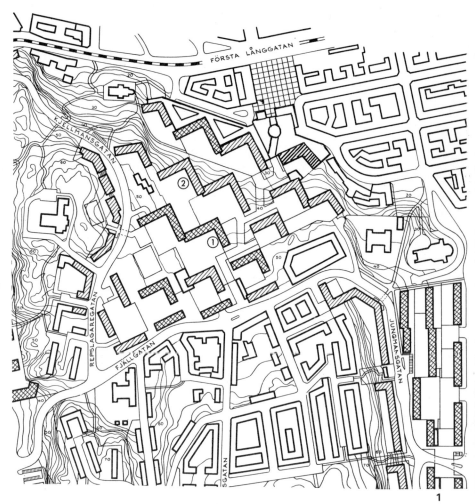

1

The new development, with
relatively low and short buildings,
rises in a rhythmic grouping up the
hill, which is crowned by Masthugg
Church. The angular shape of the
buildings is conditioned by the
ground and the terraced
construction selected. The design
and grouping of the buildings has
also produced intelligent use of

space with good sun and shelter
conditions.

The area is well-provided with
playgrounds for the smaller children.
For the older children, however, the
situation is not quite so favourable,
but the nearness of the Slottsskogs
park has been considered to
compensate in some degree for this
lack. The area contains 1,007 flats.

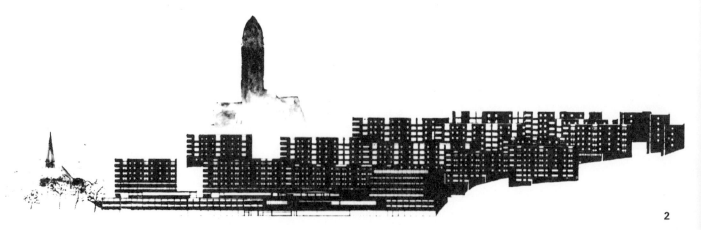

2

3

4

1 Plan showing situation
2 The development seen against the
   Masthugg Church
3 Model of the development
4 Sketch showing the landscaping of the area

WHILE WAITING FOR RENEWAL

The older town will continue to be the environment of childhood and adolescence for new generations of children, in spite of all the chaos that our day and age has introduced, with its motor traffic and car parks. It is therefore necessary to do the best we can with a situation which may sometimes appear impossible. To sit contentedly while awaiting redevelopment and better times is scarcely acceptable. Let us remember the United Nations Declaration, Principle 7 : "The child shall have full opportunity for play and recreation, which should be directed to the same purpose as education". If we cannot give the child all that it has a right to claim, we must at least give it all that we can reasonably provide. The possible, future redevelopment of old towns by no means relieves us of responsibility for their present problems. There are many possibilities if we look around for inspiration ! It is initiative, not opportunity, that is sometimes lacking.

Amsterdam's good example

In its central area, Amsterdam is a very densely populated city with high land prices and a great lack of playgrounds for children. Since the end of the Second World War, however, a redevelopment programme has been carried out to bring improvement where possible. A large number of playgrounds have been provided. These are usually quite simple playgrounds, many of them very small, but the total effort and effect is impressive. The best use has been made of the resources available. Accessible—even temporary—open spaces in the town area have been utilized; a corner here, an empty site there, a wide pavement, a square, a length of street, etc.

What has been achieved in Amsterdam should be possible for almost any town with a similar need.

1

2

3

1   Temporary playground, Zeedijk
2   Volleyball on Museumplein
3   Temporary playground, Dijkstraat

London Play Parks

Layout

As far as possible, the London play parks are sited adjacent to the usual park playgrounds with their traditional fixed equipment such as slides, roundabouts and swings. This arrangement has the advantage not only of giving children an alternative form of play close by, but also gives ready access to children's lavatories and wet weather shelters that are normally provided at playgrounds. The play parks usually cover about two acres, and are often divided by woodland fencing into as many as five sections. One is called the "adventure" area where boys and girls can build "dens" of all kinds made from odd pieces of timber, larch poles and sheets of old canvas. There is a toddlers' area, usually equipped with a simple sand pit, and toys are provided, suitable for children from five to eight years. In this section is a hutted building, which is not only the headquarters of the play park, but is also used by the children in wet weather to continue such activities as painting, drawing, modelling or puppet making.

A third section is known as the quiet area. Here, children can dress

2

up, invent and act out plays entirely spontaneously, do drawing and painting, play ludo, draughts, snakes and ladders, chess, and in fact all quiet games.

The remaining two areas are set aside for formal games. One for girls and the other for boys, although there is frequently an interchange between the two.

Staff

Each play park is staffed with a regular team of four experienced play leaders, the senior of whom is regarded as the guiding spirit of the play park. His staff consists of a deputy senior play leader and two women, one of whom is used to handling very young children, and the other whose experience lies more with older girls and their needs. The senior play leader arranges the alternating duties of the staff, as the whole team is never on duty at the same time.

The senior play leader usually selects three boys and three girls to act as monitors. They issue equipment, record their issues in a book, and see that all material is accounted for at the end of the session.

One o'clock clubs

In the summer of 1964 an experimental scheme was started in two play parks in Lambeth to provide special facilities for children under five, and to give a respite to busy mothers by engaging experienced staff to take care of the children should the mother wish to relax nearby.

The experiment was immediately successful and the Parks and Smallholdings Committee have now agreed to increase the number of "1 o'clock clubs", as they have come to be known, siting them within existing play parks.

Each club is staffed with a team of three: a senior play leader, an assistant and a trainee. The presence of the staff in no way prevents mothers from playing with their children if they wish, but in any case they must remain within the play park area throughout the session. The staff have been carefully selected, not only for their skill in handling young children, but also for their understanding of the problems and diffculties experienced by young mothers, many of whom live a considerable distance from their own parents and often feel lonely and isolated.

1

3

Equipment and activities

A wide range of suitable play equipment is provided. Supplies of drawing paper, discarded posters, gummed paper shapes, coloured pencils and plasticine are always available; other equipment consists of Wendy houses, hobby horses, dolls and dolls' cots, sand buckets, rakes and spades, coloured hoops, tea-sets, trucks and trolleys. Collapsible canvas beds and blankets are also provided. The outward expression of a child's imagination takes many forms, and dressing-up games play an important part. To meet this need a selection of dressing-up clothes is always available to the children.

Time of opening

The clubs are open from 1 p.m. to 5.30 p.m. each weekday, from Easter to the end of September.

1 Play can be achievement, too
2 A 'quiet area' section and play leader
3 Workers and watchers in the adventure area
4 One o'clock clubs are for the under fives

4

Notting Hill Adventure Playground, London

The playground is in a densely populated and underprivileged part of North Kensington on a site of just over a third of an acre (1300 square metres). The scheme consists of a playground for school age children, and a separate area for under fives by the playground building.

The school-age playground
The main playground is divided into three sections, the Adventure Area, the Ball Game Area and the Garden. The largest and most important of these is the Adventure Area which is the starting point and the heart of the whole scheme. The existing ground surface of old asphalt and earth has been retained in this section.

The ball game area is divided from the rest of the playground by a wall of concrete blocks, with the excavated material from the building piled against it and shaped and graded. This bank was then surfaced with sprayed concrete on steel mesh.

In the most secluded corner a quite ambitious garden was planned and then dropped, partly due to cost and partly to give the children the opportunity of making the garden themselves.

The under fives area
This area being on the south-west side of the building is the most sunny and sheltered part and has a sandpit and a paddling pool with paved

1

2

3

4

surround. The central area has a
smooth asphalt surface and is
used by the toddlers with their
wheeled toys and for their games.
The area is intended to be used by
older children as well, but for quieter
activities than would be carried on in
the adventure area; table tennis and
other games could be played here on
summer evenings. A terrace has been
built along one side for sitting on; this
was intended to be filled with a good
topsoil for the children to grow seeds
and plants.

The roof
This is part of the playground and has
been planned with areas for play on
different levels, one of which is a
turret. The roof is intended for the
older children and can be reached
only by climbing a steep ladder. The
slide is fun and also satisfies the
authorities as a quick means of
escape. A further description of the
house is given on page 178.

Fencing the site
The fencing was carried out before
the playground work. A 4 metre
(13 feet) fence was built of concrete

0   5   10   15 m

N

terrace
for
garden
plots

pool   under fives' area

paving

seat   sand pit   sunken
roof

pavilion roof

ladder

turret

slide

bank

retaining
wall   •lamp

ball game area   adventure area

•lamp

garden

Telford Road

Wornington Road

5

1, 2   Adventure play area
3, 4   'Under fives' area
5   Site plan

E

7

8

planks, high enough to keep the balls inside, and solid enough to make the playground into a world apart. This is important because the adventure area is inevitably very untidy. Also the children do not want to be watched by outsiders.

A commentary
Notting Hill Adventure Playground is interesting from several points of view. It is an excellent example of the fact that the size of an area is not of decisive importance for a good playground. On one third of an acre

a playground has been created which fully merits the praise it has received. It has a warm and protective atmosphere, far superior to any I have seen elsewhere. The high wall which limits the playworld—or rather shuts out an adult world which is duller in Notting Hill than in most areas—is a valuable addition. The happiness and activity within the walls are in sharp contrast to the depressing surroundings.

The relationship that exists between play indoors and out-of-doors is ideal, for the children are able to move in and out quite freely. The house is an integral part of the playground and the border between the one and the other is hardly noticeable, even if the building itself is rather closed off.

A demarcation between games for

6

9

13

10

12

11

14

smaller and larger children has, of course, been drawn but it seems to exist during morning hours only, when the younger children's section is used as a kindergarten. And what a kindergarten! I have never seen more rubbish in one and the same place, but there again I have never seen a richer play society, more absorbed play or greater freedom anywhere else. There is no institutional atmosphere, no system for system's sake, no occupational therapy. The whole atmosphere tends towards self-initiative and new discoveries, and adventure seems to be constantly lying in wait.

Notting Hill Adventure Playground is an issue for discussion, a challenge to the tedious and pre-arranged, an expression of trust in a child's natural ability to create its own order out of chaos. The playground shocks many visitors deeply, but to others it is a liberation to find, at last, a playground where everything other than play itself is considered completely unimportant.

6, 7, 8, 9   Adventure play area
10, 11, 12, 13, 14   'Under fives' playground

67

Tokyo builds playgrounds

In the city of Tokyo, which in 1960 had an area of 569 square km (220 square miles) and a population of over 10 million, there are open spaces equivalent to less than 0·51 square metres (0·61 square yard) per citizen. This compares unfavourably with :

    Osaka 1·10 square metres
               (1·3 square yards).
    Kyoto 1·19 square metres
               (1·42 square yards).
    London 9·2 square metres
               (11·00 square yards).
    New York 11·9 square metres
               (14·23 square yards).

Open spaces in Tokyo number 375, with a total area of 443 hectares (1,094 acres). This total is made up of 73 parks and neighbourhood parks of 245 hectares (605 acres), 14 playgrounds of 106 hectares (262 acres) and 288 children's playgrounds of 71 hectares (175 acres). Thus there are almost no large parks or neighbourhood parks in the crowded sections of the town. In such districts, playgrounds are in effect the only open spaces, so children of all ages are obliged to spend their leisure time there, while youths and adults have almost no other open spaces for active recreation. For this reason, the

1

children's playgrounds are officially named "small public parks" and are open for the public in general, day and night, although furnished specifically for children. Such children's playgrounds average 0·25 hectares (0·6 acres) in area in the redeveloped centre of the city and are sited about 300 metres apart. They are completely unsupervised. As yet there are no recreation or play leaders, or playground managers, usually not even a watchman.

In such conditions the difficulties are obvious : each playground has to cater for a great many children of all ages ; keep them there for long periods despite overcrowding, rather than on the streets ; and try to provide the high degree of safety demanded by the parents despite the absence of offical supervision and the presence of older children, youths and adults.

Text by Kuro Kaneko and Mary Mitchell

2

5

3

6

4

7

1 Slide and play sculpture at Aato children's playground
2 Ornamental pond in front of the art gallery, temporarily used for bathing
3 Seika children's playground
4, 6 Teppozu, Tokyo
5 Triya-minami
7 Aato children's playground

Five playgrounds in Central Park, New York

Richard Dattner's well-known playground on 67th Street, New York, is the first of a series of five playgrounds that it is planned to lay out in Central Park. This project stems from the chaotic play conditions in the surrounding areas of the City, and from the need to utilize fully the open spaces available.

The Dattner playground has been financed privately and has been named the Estee and Joseph Lauder playground after its donors. It has an enclosed layout with beautiful old trees which have been skillfully incorporated into the playground. A low, winding concrete wall forms the boundary between a peripheral hard-surfaced play area and an inner soft, sandy area. The winding movement of the wall forms small, intimate play recesses and the fine-filtered sand from Long Island beach is soft and pleasant for play purposes. The equipment is excellent and the design leaves little to be desired; what is perhaps missing is the loose building material that could make the playground really creative.

1

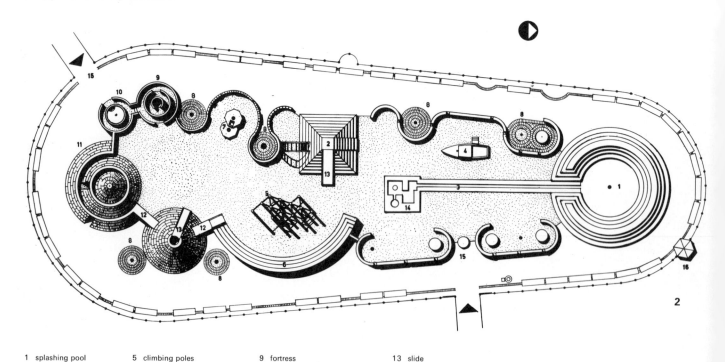

2

1	splashing pool	5	climbing poles	9	fortress	13	slide
2	climbing roof	6	amphitheatre	10	entrance tower	14	paddling pools
3	water channel	7	tree houses	11	mound within a mound	15	entrance
4	boat	8	tree pit	12	tunnel	16	pump house

4

3

1 Playground seen from the south. In the fore-
   ground, the mound in a mound
2 Plan
3 A maze of concentric concrete 'fortress'
   walls at the entrance from the south
4 Splashing pool: the water is carried along a
   shallow channel before draining from a
   series of shallow pools and islands

71

Portable playgrounds in New York

The portable playgrounds developed for the Department of Parks by landscape architect Paul Friedberg are an ingenious system of modular play equipment which requires no foundations, can be bolted together, is quickly assembled and dismantled, and easily transferred from one site to another. In fact, the elements—pipe frame and concrete modules, lengths of wood, pipe and cable units—can be stockpiled and used by any designer. Temporarily vacant lots, some as small as 6 × 22·5 metres (20 × 75 feet) are being converted into play areas for a two- or three-year period. A welcome respite in crowded areas.

1

*1, 2, 3, 4 The playgrounds as erected on
various sites*

29th Street, "vest pocket" park, New York

Landscape architects: M. Paul Friedberg & Associates.

The vest pocket park at East 29th Street and Second Avenue is both playground and nature study centre : an innovation and a possible prototype for other parks, each park focusing on a different facet of natural science. At 29th Street, the centre is a planetarium, placed below ground level, its dome a pyramid for climbing, so that no play area is sacrificed. Planetarium and play area work together educationally.

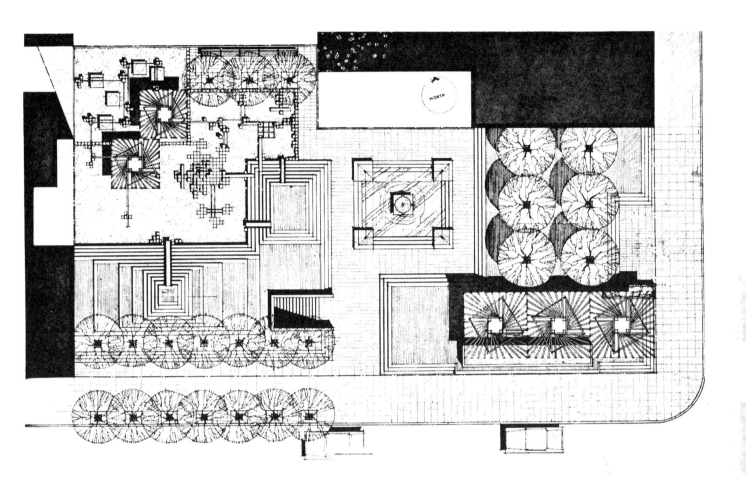

Festival Streets in New York

The purpose of the project is to provide neighbourhoods throughout the city with some tools for enriching the potential of their environment. Each street on which the units are housed will be blocked off as a Festival Street during the summer months. The units will be planned and designed by an architect and an artist working directly with the community concerned. The units will act in two ways: (1) to inject into the street a sense of expectation and elegance by the use of banners, greenery, and sitting areas designed to remain as an enhancement to the street for the duration of the summer. (2) to provide building elements such as platforms, screens and display units which may be interlocked in a variety of ways to meet particular requirements. Through thoughtful and imaginative design of these units, it is hoped to create a new kind of public architecture, one which comes close to theatrical design in that it will "come alive" as a creative function of the action within it.

The semi-permanent units will establish the street as a place with a particular identity—for a place is in itself an excuse for gathering.

The following is a list of components to be considered:
1. *Entrances*, such as archways.
2. *Vertical structures* of scaffolding placed at intervals along the street, making it possible to hang banners, flags, light and sound equipment, and overhead wiring.
3. *Surfaces* which are pleasant to the feet and easily cleaned. Multi-coloured pieces of synthetic material laid in patterns to form various shapes and spaces.
4. *Portable fountains* tapped from a fire hydrant.
5. *Plants*, "Street Gardens" in pots or boxes.
6. *Benches,* joined to form sitting areas.
7. Collapsible *sun-roofs* or *umbrellas* along with the "Street Gardens" as an essential complement to sitting areas.
8. Colourful *kiosks* or *refreshment carts* leased for concessionairing. (The "hot dog man" on Puerto Rican streets is sometimes the local clown and raconteur.)
9. *Tables and chairs* to form a kind of sidewalk cafe.

Activities
1. Craft and art workshops for children.
2. Classes for adults.
3. Story Telling, Group Discussion.
4. Street Games and athletics.
5. Portable mini-playground.

The Festival Street Components will open up the grid pattern on which New York is planned, to provide a breathing space in everyday movement of people through the city. As a gathering place it parallels the ancient city piazza. Unlike the piazza and modern equivalents such as Lincoln Center, it will have not one central focus but a series of centers, permitting a flow of simultaneous activities.

Fulton Mall, Fresno, California

Architects: Eckbo, Dean, Austin &
Williams.

Many shopping streets are today
converted into pedestrian streets and
the success is far too obvious,
commercially and environmentally,
to be questioned. Fulton Mall in
Fresno is one of the many examples
it would have been possible to
illustrate in various countries.

Whatever is possible in a busy
shopping street, should also be
possible in an old housing area
where, in the past, the roads were
often the only playground for
children. On such roads the motor
vehicle is the intruder, not the
playing children, and this should be
remembered in any discussion of
priorities. A car owner can be
expected to walk a reasonable
distance to a car park. The child, on
the other hand, will play outside his
own front door, however we plan.

1

2

1   Fulton Mall as a traffic route
2   As a pedestrian and play street

ONE-FAMILY HOUSING

A major advantage of one-family houses compared with other types of dwellings is without doubt the garden, the private outside space which, in addition to other uses, serves to some extent as a playground. Indeed, one might be inclined to believe that this type of housing would need no other playground, and where older areas with large gardens are concerned this may well be so. However, most modern estates of one-family houses have comparatively small plots, and in such areas playgrounds are certainly needed as a complement to the gardens, which are often far too variegated and well-kept to function as recreation areas. Indeed, the lack of meeting places and amenities, especially for older children, is often more critical in such instances than in an area of blocks of flats. A football in the road soon lands in the next garden. The first time this happens it is ignored, perhaps the next time too, but irritation is soon caused and before one realises it good-neighbourly relations are endangered. The lack of a space for ball games can be sufficent to divide an area of one-family houses into two camps, with spiteful attacks from both sides.

The accident rate among playing children is often high

The comparatively high accident rate among playing children in many one-family housing estates may be due to the fact that the street is so often the only community area, and serves as an obvious playground for children. The sporadic traffic gives a false sense of safety, which blunts attention, and parked cars obscure the view of children rushing out. Abundant vegetation in the gardens often protrudes into the road and can be an added hazard. A differentiation of motor traffic, walking and playing traffic is consequently no less important in a one-family housing estate than elsewhere.

Group developments

A dense group development of one-family houses is an interesting alternative to the traditional concept. Indeed, the concentration gives not only economic advantages but, to a great extent, environmental advantages too. The gain in space, for example, makes it possible to provide communal areas for play and recreation within a reasonable walking distance. The small intimate garden space in, say, an atrium house, complemented by a common play area is preferable, for many people, to a large and work-demanding garden, with the children, nevertheless, so often restricted to the road for their communal play. Another great advantage of concentrated group development is that the traffic problem can be more readily solved in a satisfactory manner.

F

Falken, Nyköping, Sweden

Architect: Leif Haking.
Landscape architects: Sven A. Hermelin & Inger Wedborn.

The Falken area at Nyköping, built in 1956, was one of the first estates of one-family houses in Sweden to have systematic traffic differentation. Garages and parking areas were beside the access routes, the rest of the area was free of cars.

Apart from 26 detached houses, the estate also includes two three-storey blocks with 37 flats in all. The internal footpaths have been designed as play paths and form a valuable complement to the estate's two playgrounds.

1 The garden as a playground
2 Play street
3 Site plan showing the system of traffic segregation

1

82

2

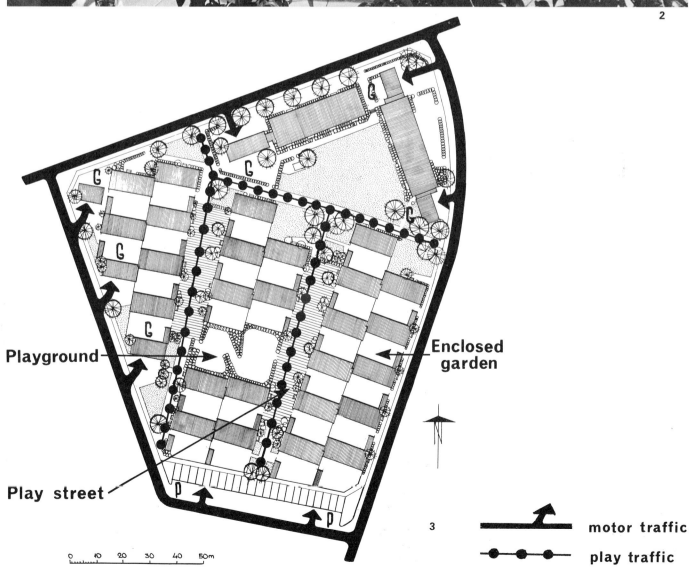

Playground

Enclosed garden

Play street

3

0 10 20 30 40 50m

— motor traffic

• • • play traffic

Oxhagen, Örebro, Sweden

Architects: WAAB White AB.

Period of construction 1964–66. The area is developed with one- and two-storey terraced houses, a total of 137 units.
Parking spaces and garages have been located at the entry to the area. Only footpaths and cycle paths lead into the area, and playgrounds for small children are connected with them. To the north, there is direct vehicle-free access to a wooded area, with recreation grounds of various kinds.

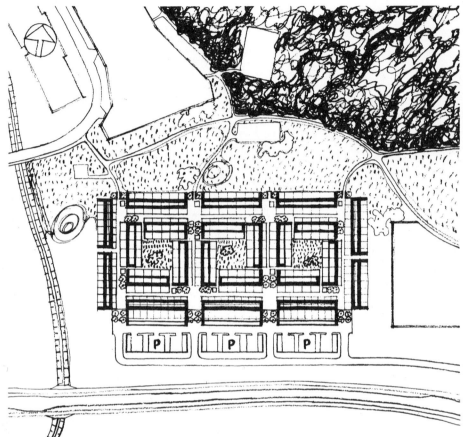

Torslanda, Gothenburg, Sweden

Architects: Jansson, Persson,
Trogard, Lilja.
Landscape architects: Lars Barnö AB.

The houses are arranged in three compact, clearly separated groups in an open landscape with well-accentuated outcrops of rock. Adjacent playgrounds of somewhat different types have been provided for the children within each group of houses. Each playground has a foundation of soft sand, with toys and play equipment all of wood. Spaces for ball games have been provided in the meadows among the groups of houses; these, together with the outcrops of rock, form the most important playgrounds for the older children.

Garaging and parking have been provided adjacent to the access road, the entire area being otherwise free of cars. Building period 1967—68.

A   playground for small children
B   ballgame area
C   playground for young children
P   parking

House
Enclosed garden

Garage

Parking

P

TORSLANDA – KUNGALV

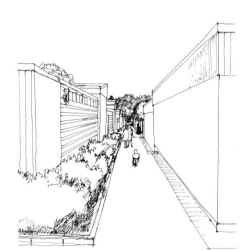

PLAYGROUNDS—PLANNING

The following standards were arrived at by the United National Technical Assistance Administration 1958 conference in Stockholm previously referred to.

1. Playgrounds for small children
A playspace for small children, with sand, grass, seats and tables, should be within sight of their homes.

2. Playgrounds for young children
In each neighbourhood and on each housing estate there should be a network of playgrounds for young children, in addition to those for very small children near their homes.

3. The comprehensive playground
For young children, teenagers and older groups, the larger comprehensive playground should be available in each neighbourhood unit and provide a wide variety of activities that can be adapted to local conditions.

Who does what ?
Is planning for play a private matter and, therefore, the concern of the owner of the development, or is it one of the functions, for which the municipality is responsible ? The answer to this question varies in different countries and, indeed,

within a country. There is in fact no general rule. In many Swedish towns a general practice has developed for the owner of the property to be responsible for the immediate vicinity and the play areas included therein, that is to say playgrounds for the younger children. The municipality, on the other hand, is responsible for the play park which is a common facility for a larger area. The private plan has usually to be submitted to the Building Committee for approval. With such a division of responsibility, co-ordination is essential to avoid the risk of duplicating projects.

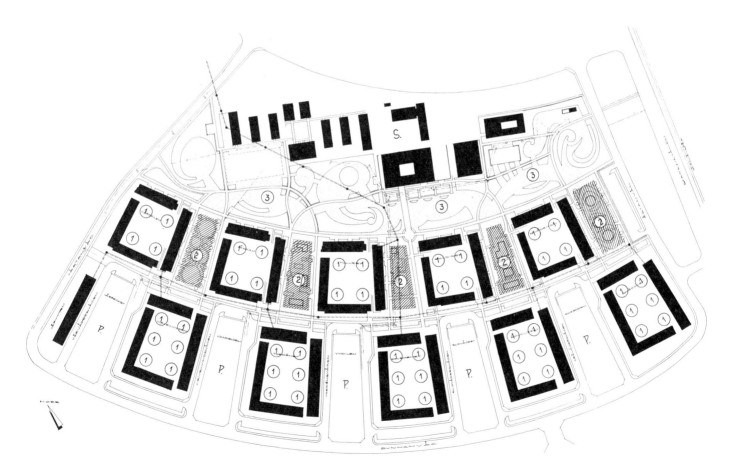

1   playgrounds for small children
2   playgrounds for young
    children
3   comprehensive playground
    (play park)
S   school
P   parking

PLAYGROUNDS FOR SMALL CHILDREN

The playworld for the younger child is the immediate neighbourhood, and should be developed with this in mind. The entrance area is the centre from which all activities radiate, so it is not possible to exclude any age group from this area, but the younger children should be the deciding factor when it comes to the planning and furnishing of equipment. Everything which carries a risk for them should be excluded. Swings and other advanced playthings may belong in the playground, but within the small child's sector they should be banned. By dividing the outdoor environment into peaceful and active sectors a greater variety is also obtained.

What younger children most need is a suitable play surface : smooth, hard surfaces for their cars, carts, bicycles, etc, soft sand surfaces for constructive activity, and grassy surfaces as well if conditions are favourable.

A feeling of space is important for well-being
Screens of suitable kinds—vegetation, ramparts, walls and hoardings—can be used to divide areas that are too large into "room" spaces of different shapes and sizes. In this way shelter from the wind and a pleasant feeling of intimacy is

2

created which is all important to well-being.

The quality of the "room" itself as a space to move about in has seldom been sufficently considered, and yet it is certainly no less important than the furnishing of equipment to which more thought is usually given.

Furnishing for "togetherness"
Equipping an area for play is not just a matter of providing playthings : it also means pleasant sitting places and a nook or corner with a table to gather around. Furnishing for play is to a great extent furnishing for "togetherness". The little group needs small hiding places where it can feel undisturbed, and since many such groups will form where there are large numbers of children, an equivalent number of hiding places is needed.

"Playgroves" for the very young
For very young children, who may stray away whenever opportunity arises, special precautions must be taken if a mother is to feel able to leave the children on their own at all. A fenced in "playgrove", sufficiently large for the child not to feel imprisoned, should be part of any courtyard. It is also important that such a playgrove should be within the dwelling's field of vision.

1

3

4

5

Spare material for play construction
Here a real difficulty begins, and is the conflict with the accepted ideas of order and tidiness. Bits of boards, wooden boxes, worn out car tyres etc, are all what we adults call rubbish, but the same ''rubbish'' lights a child's eyes and offers untold adventure.

As far as the small child is concerned, only simple and harmless materials are needed, so serious difficulties need not arise. This is not a matter of a building playground in its usual sense—nails and hammers, etc, are not called for. That is why it should be acceptable, even close to the dwellings where, of course, it

should be sited. Such a building corner can be arranged as a closed section, fenced off with hedges or screens. The screen should not be so high that it prevents an adult from having a full view, but it should be sufficiently tall to give the children a feeling of seclusion.

Sand is a suitable base and there should be enough to serve as building material as well.

Finally it must be pointed out that several small building corners are better than one large one. The ''rubbish'' will tend to spread outside the planned areas, but as large amounts are not involved, a daily clean up should be sufficent.

1 *Smooth hard surfaces are important for children's wheeled toys*
2 *A pleasant feeling of intimacy can be created by correct planting*
3 *The entrance area is the centre for outdoor activities of young children*
4 *Wood is a good material for equipment*
5 *Benches and tables are just as necessary as any other play equipment*

8

6

9

7

10

13

11

12

6, 9   A great variety of surfaces is desirable
8   Special provision must be made for very
     small children, who may stray away
7, 10, 11, 12   Little hiding places are needed,
     where the small group can feel secure or
     where a child can take refuge to play alone
13   In a playground for small children provi-
     sion must be made for the mother

Play courtyard, Råda Säteri, Sweden

Landscape architect:
Carl-Vilhelm Sundin AB.

The courtyard is situated between
parallel rows of three-storey buildings.
The long "street" has been divided by
means of trellis work and vegetation
to create comprehensive space
forms. Playgrounds for small
children have been placed adjacent
to these trellises, and the whole
courtyard functions, in fact, as a
play area. The surface is of asphalt
and concrete slabs forming a
pattern. The quiet play area, which
has been equipped for the needs of
the smaller children, is complemented
by more active playgrounds near by.

1 site plan
2 play yard and trellising
3 plan of play yard

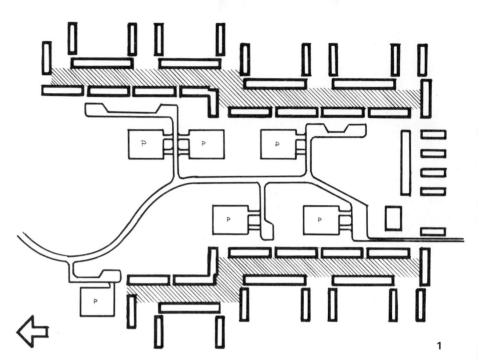

1

2

94

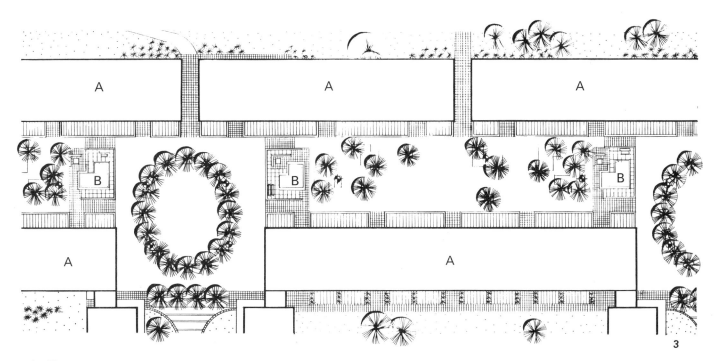

A *Houses*
B *Playgrounds*

PLAYGROUNDS FOR YOUNG CHILDREN

The playground for young children is a play area within the immediate neighbourhood, but incorporated into the environment in such a manner that it lies outside the very small child's radius of movement, and can be equipped for somewhat more advanced play. Perhaps its most important purpose, however, is its function as a meeting point. Inviting corners with benches and tables, therefore, form an important part of the equipment. It is an advantage for the young children's playground to have the character of a sand playground, perhaps with play equipment in the sand. A smaller, fenced-in area for ball games is a valuable complement. If this is given minimum dimensions, perhaps no more than 15 × 25 m (50 × 80 ft), it is made less attractive to the older children who will prefer the larger play park for this type of play. Maximum walking distance from the houses : 150 metres (130 yd).

Playground in Hansestrasse Bremen, West Germany

Planning: Gartenbauamt, Bremen.

The playground in Hansestrasse is one of my most memorable playground experiences and is still, to me, something of an ideal as a congenial and pleasant "playroom". The play area is well protected from the wind by the generous vegetation surrounding it. Unfortunately none of the photographs shown do it complete justice.

The playground consists mainly of a generous area of soft, splendid sand in which are various kinds of play equipment. Only the communication surfaces are hard. The playground has a separate section for the smallest children, with toilets and a protective roof against rain and strong sunshine.

If anything is lacking it is, perhaps, loose building material. Imagine this playground with, perhaps, less play equipment but with some hundreds of wooden building bricks instead, and a few simple constructions on which to build. I have no doubt that the playground would swarm with children.

1

2

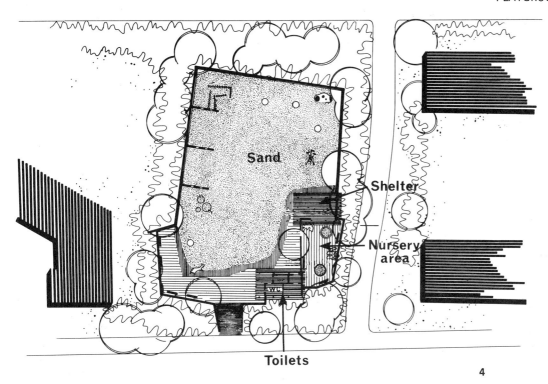

Sand

Shelter

Nursery area

WC

Toilets

4

1, 2   The sandplay area
3   Aerial view
4   Plan

3

Playground in Deckerstrasse Stuttgart, West Germany

Planning: Gartenbauamt, Stuttgart.

The playground is surrounded by traffic routes on all sides and this factor is, of course, most undesirable. However, in the old, confined sectors of a town there is rarely any choice, and one must make the best of an almost impossible situation by utilizing the few favourable resources available.

Gartenbauamt in Stuttgart are ambitious where planning for play is concerned, and even from this not very promising open space they have succeeded in creating a meeting point serving almost all ages, from small children in the sandpit to old gentlemen at the chessboard or at the round table for the Germans' favourite card game of "skat". The heavy screening from the surroundings gives a sense of seclusion, which will be even stronger in a few years' time when the vegetation has grown.

1

1 *View of the playground from one of the flats in Worishofenerstrasse*
2 *Climbing bridge*
3 *Plan*

2

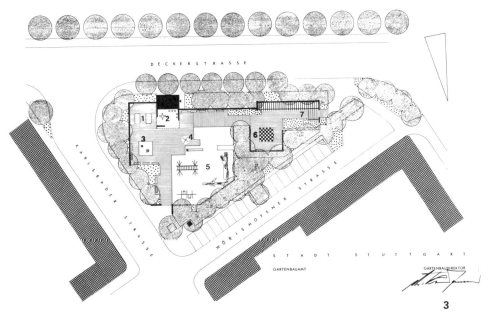

1 table tennis
2 card tables
3 sand pit
4 roundabout
5 sand area (various equipment)
6 chessboard
7 pergola

3

Playground at Toyoskiki, Tokyo

Landscape architect: Kuro Kaneko.

The main part of the playground has a metal "box" framework where various equipment such as swings, climbing ropes, etc, is grouped. The framework provides shade when required by the addition of matting.

Another notable feature of the playground is an exciting concrete spire for climbing and sliding down.

1   The concrete climbing 'spire'
2   Climbing and swinging boxed frames
3   General view of the playground

Teppozu Children's Playground, Tokyo

Landscape architect: Kuro Kaneko.

The playground was opened in 1935 but redesigned and reconstructed in 1962. Sited near a primary school, it caters for an average of 200 children, rising to a maximum of 400, at any one time.

One of its most exciting features is the mound surfaced in concrete, with a gently sloping face which is backed on the steep side with rounded stones, concrete plugs and metal hoops, enabling children to climb up one side and slide down the other.

1 Plan of site
2 The mound with its climbing stones and slide face is an exciting feature

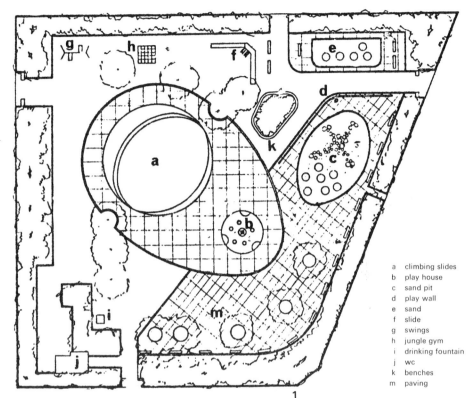

a climbing slides
b play house
c sand pit
d play wall
e sand
f slide
g swings
h jungle gym
i drinking fountain
j wc
k benches
m paving

1

2

Chamberlain Gardens, Birmingham

Landscape architect: Mary Mitchell, FILA.

Mary Mitchell's playgrounds are well known far beyond England, and Chamberlain Gardens is only one example among many which could represent her work. Superficially they all appear to be similar, but if studied more closely it soon becomes clear that they derive from the conditions of the location, and that all are different. What is common to all her playgrounds is the fact that she works with earth forms : shapes placed around the landscape so that it becomes transformed, to achieve the play environment she is seeking.

In Chamberlain Gardens, the presence of some fine trees made the conditions unusually good. Trees that had to be sacrificed for the housing development survive in one form or another as parts of the playground.

1

2

104

3

1, 3   To withstand heavy wear, the mounds
       were sprayed with a cement compound on
       a reinforcing mesh
2   Hard-surfaced area with a broad slope to a
       lower level

105

Playground in Karl Örnsgatan, Helsingborg Sweden

Landscape architects: Parks Department, Helsingborg.

The playground is on slightly sloping ground within a mixed development of detached houses and blocks of flats. The organized sector of the playground consists of a sand section equipped with play tables and climbing frame, and of a hard surfaced area with various play equipment. Adjacent to this is a grass area where the vegetation is arranged with a view to providing quiet play recesses. In the organized sector, the vegetation has been planted in raised beds. The reason for this is partly practical—to give the new plants a chance to survive the heavy wear—and partly the desire to give the playground a sheltered and cosy character. The walls of the sand pit already form a certain amount of confined spaces for the children.

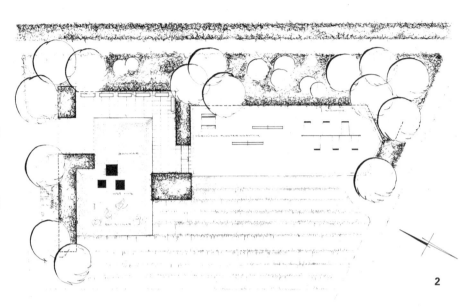

2

1

3

1   The playground in its first year. Small huts for quiet play
2   Plan of organized sector of the playground
3   After 5 years the vegetation has closed in and makes a sheltered playroom

Storängen, Helsingborg, Sweden

Landscape architects: Parks
Department, Helsingborg.

The playground is completely
dominated by a large, oval, sand
depression surrounded by a hard
track for the small children's cycles
and cars. The sand area has been
equipped with an old, discarded
sailing boat, a slide and a play table
with plenty of wooden building
bricks. The playground is fenced by a
free-growing hedge which, over the
years, has been provided with various
openings to the surrounding play
area.

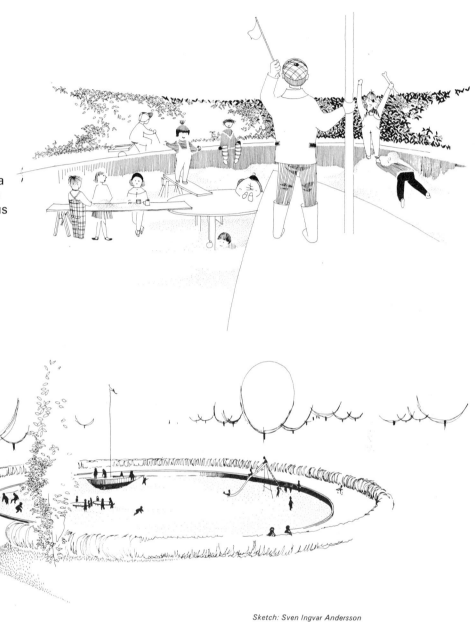

Sketch: Sven Ingvar Andersson

107

Trumman, Helsingborg, Sweden

Landscape architects: Parks Department, Helsingborg.

The area of the playground is just under a quarter of an acre, in a mixed development of old one-family houses and new houses with a number of flats.

The limited area, and the wish to provide at least something for the older children, has made it necessary to divide the area into two sections: one section consists of a fenced-in area for ball games, which converts into a skating rink in winter; the other is a sand playground with hard play surfaces around it and various play equipment. The relatively large sand surface has been divided into big and small sections surrounded by "walls" of wood at various heights to give the effect of "rooms".

1 Plan of the playground
2 A popular swing in the sand area
3, 4 Low, wooden walls give a sheltered and cosy atmosphere
5 General view of the area

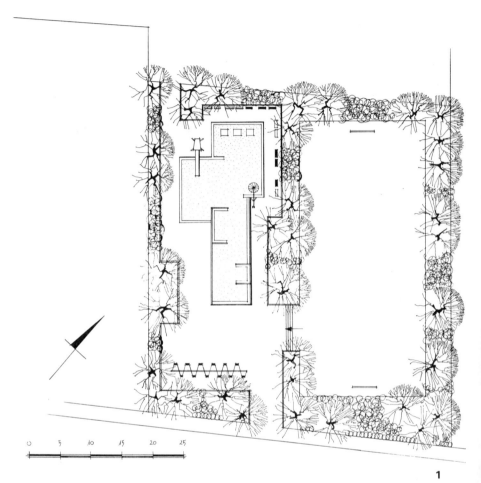

1

2

3

4

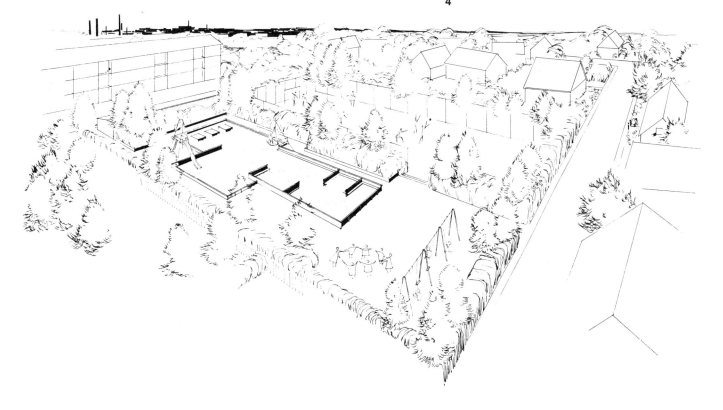

5

THE COMPREHENSIVE PLAYGROUND
(Play Park)

The play park is an active and comparatively new type of park. Ideally, it should contain layouts for different age groups, i.e., not only for children and adults, but for the age groups in between for which we often fail to provide in traditional parks. In such a play park, tennis courts and courts for other ball games—they could be of the simplest kind—are just as essential as swings and sandpits ; and resting places for the aged are no less important than layouts for active pursuits.

The play park is a local amenity which should act as the centre of a neighbourhood. Its size is normally based on a population of between 3,000 and 5,000, but in my estimation the number is of secondary importance, a more vital factor being the walking distance from home. The closer one lives to the play park the more importance it assumes. Children on the edge of the catchment area go there less often, and those who live beyond a certain radius hardly ever go at all. Investigations carried out in

Stockholm have shown that the walking distance from a play park should not exceed 400 metres (440 yds), but in my own experience 300 metres (330 yds) is more realistic. However, there are many factors which influence the size of the catchment area : the topography of the landscape is one. If the destination lies at the bottom of a comfortable downhill stretch the way seems shorter and the end nearer than if one has to struggle up hill to get there. A play park in the bottom of a valley consequently has a

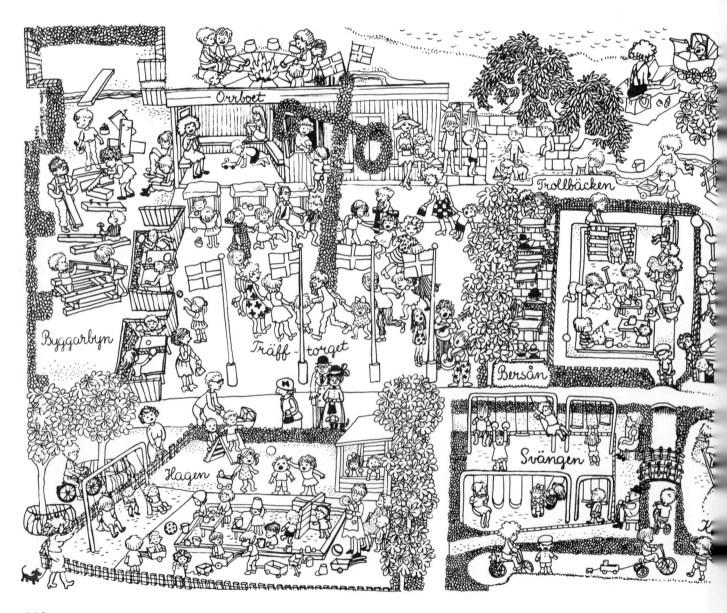

larger catchment area than one that is high and hard of access. Proper location in relation to the town as a whole is decisive. A convenient link with an area's favourite play stretches (and the latter often relate to the placing of schools and shops) gives a play park vitality and increases its attraction. Likewise, an unfavourable situation can greatly reduce the size of a catchment area even if the layout is excellent.

Relatively large variations in terms of area between different projects are apparent. As a general rule 15,000 square metres (about 4 acres) are adequate. With a larger area the chances of giving the layout a more park-like character increase, because grass areas must be relatively large in order to resist wear. If size is restricted, hard surfaces should be planned. As it is essential to have short walking distances and a central position, one often has to economize on space and try to get as much as possible into the restricted area. With very concentrated layouts, therefore, it will often be found necessary to construct a series of "rooms" defined by boards, hedges or banks, each section being designed for a specific type of activity whilst at the same time retaining, within the framework of the "room", the greatest possible flexibility. The aim is not to force the children into pens according to age and play stage, but to create a rich variation of environments from which to choose. A concentrated layout has the advantage that everything is near at hand: after being tired out in the playing field, for instance, the child could settle down, perhaps around a table, for a rest, possibly make new friends, and soon be on the move again.

A meeting place

One of a play park's most important functions is to act as a meeting place for the neighbourhood, and this naturally needs consideration right from the town planning stage. A meeting place should be strategically positioned at the centre of events. Design and equipment are other important factors and provision must be made for social intercourse as well as active pursuits. An intimate corner with seats and tables and a good windshelter will be further enhanced by a roof, and perhaps a heater for cold evenings. Electric heating is becoming a common feature in outdoor restaurants, on pavements, etc, so why not have it in play parks as well? The opportunity of buying a hot frankfurter, a hamburger or a Coca-Cola would further add to the feeling of well-being and should not be impossible to organize.

Sketch: Ilon Wikland

Three Play Parks in Helsingborg

Landscape architects: Parks Department, Helsingborg.

During the 'fifties, a special type of play park was developed at Helsingborg, which has since been followed elsewhere. The source of inspiration was the adventure playground at Emdrup outside Copenhagen, which was opened at the beginning of the 'forties. The aim was to attempt to incorporate this form of playground within the general playground planning of a housing development.

In the play parks at Helsingborg, the adventure playground is incorporated as one of many play alternatives. In some parks it has been surrounded by a high wooden fence, in others by vegetation only. Another feature of these play parks is the relatively large sections provided for sand play; these include various kinds of play equipment such as a play table, climbing facilities, slides, play houses, etc.

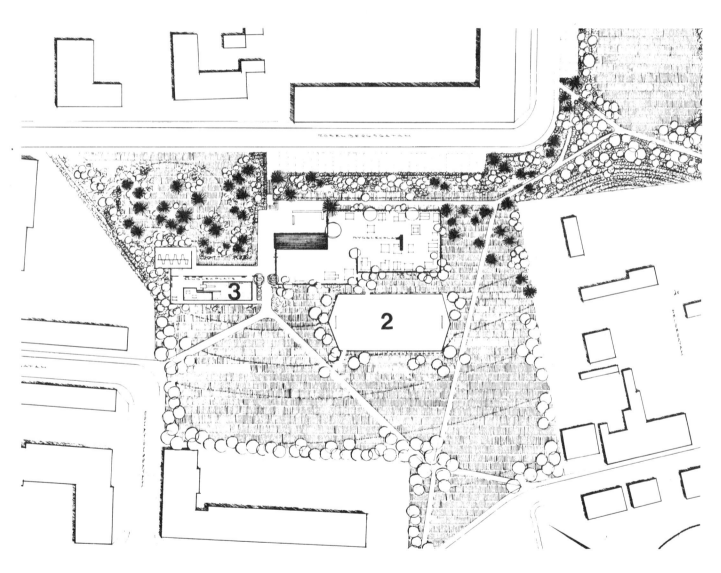

Play areas are on different levels of the terraced slope

1 adventure area
2 ball games
3 sand play

1 ROSENBERGSGATAN

This play park was the first of the
new parks. It is situated on a
somewhat inclined site, and apart
from the fenced-in adventure
playground it also contains a large
sand sector, a space with swings, a
playground building, an area for ball
games and some grass areas.

It is worth noticing that the ball
game area, which originally lay about
100 metres outside the play park,
was little used until it was directly
connected to the other play facilities.
This step was taken because ball
kicking had become widespread
throughout the entire play park. The
new area for all games quickly solved
this problem. The example
emphasizes the importance of
concentration in play planning. The
various units should be situated
sufficently near to one another for one
activity to be easily transferred into
another.

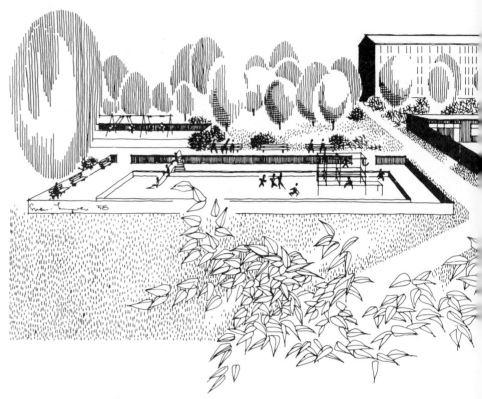

1

1, 3 *The enclosed adventure play area serves
as an ice rink in winter*
2 *Sketch of the area*
4 *A supply of wooden boxes is soon transformed into a town community*

Sketch: Sven-Ingvar Andersson

2

3

4

115

5

5, 6   The adventure playground

6

2 ELINEBERG

The housing estate is built around an enchanting view over Öresund and the Danish coast. The development consists mainly of three-floor detached buildings with a notable group of 12-storey tower blocks in the northern part of the area.

The play park is dominated by the large playing field adjacent to the buildings. The more organized section has been located on the steep slope which borders the area on the west. Some terracing has been done and opportunities for play have been provided at various levels on the slope.

1 Site plan
2 Natural playground on the slope bordering the play area

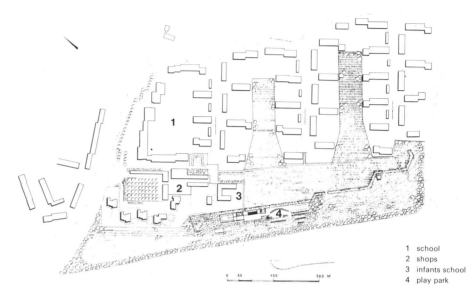

1 school
2 shops
3 infants school
4 play park

1

2

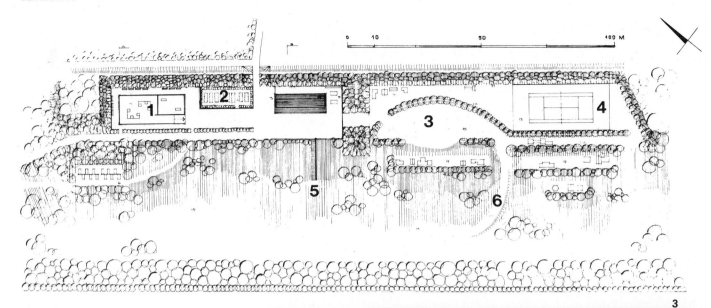

1 sand play
2 flower garden
3 adventure playground
4 tennis court
5 slide
6 track down slope

3 Plan of the playground
4 Slide down the slope
5 View from the adventure playground
   towards the sand section
6 A happy community
7 Sand play section
8 Looking toward the sand play area

3 RINGSTORP

The play park is situated on level ground, and the division into sections has been effected by earth mounds planted with suitable trees and shrubs. The grounds are arranged around a central play court which incorporates the playground building; the latter is combined with a day nursery.

To give the children a vantage-point and to provide a toboggan run for winter games, a hill of excavated earth about four metres (15 ft) high has been erected. This also serves as the starting point of a slide.

1

2

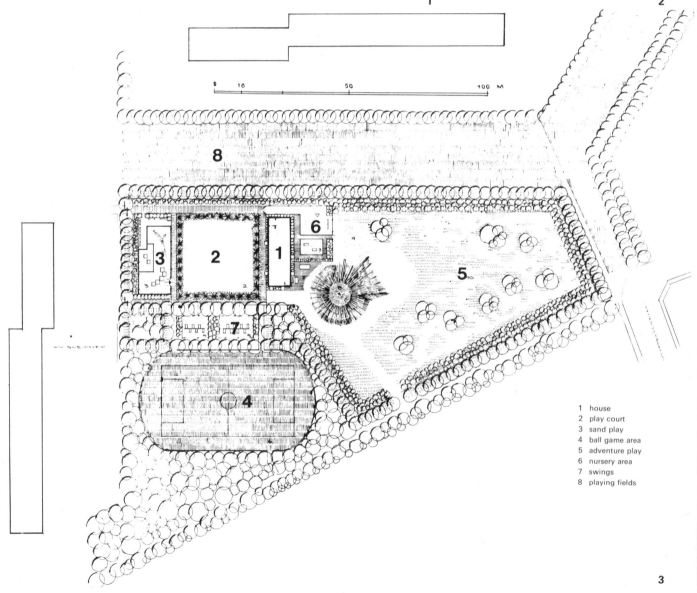

1 house
2 play court
3 sand play
4 ball game area
5 adventure play
6 nursery area
7 swings
8 playing fields

3

5

4

1, 2   Central play court
3   Plan of the play park
4   Sand play sector
5   The slide on the hill

Play parks in West Frölunda, Gothenburg

The district is located south-west of the city of Gothenburg and has a total population of about 50,000. The housing units have been planned and erected in several stages during the period 1961–1968, mainly in the form of multi-family houses. Each unit has its own play park, generally situated in connection with the schools and within walking distance of all dwellings. The pedestrian pathways are in most cases completely separated from motor traffic.

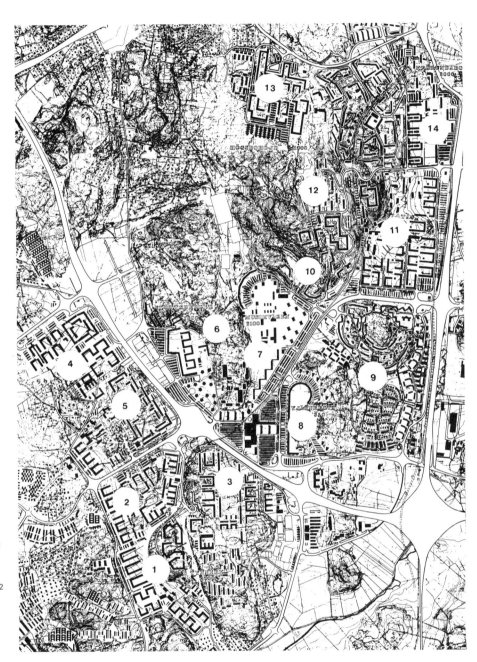

TURKOSEN AND OPALEN

Both play parks are situated within the western part of South Tynnered in an area which was originally level and fertile arable land. In contrast to Topasen, the play park is consequently an artifical product. The park environment has been created by planting, the play spaces being shaped according to their different functions and co-ordinated into an entity.

The backbone of both developments is formed by a tree-planted pedestrian street which acts as a connecting link between residences —school—shops—playgrounds and a tram service. The avenue is almost one kilometre long and is planted with horse chestnuts. Trees of this type have great advantages in such a setting : they provide chestnuts for the children to play with and for making things ; they can withstand heavy pruning when the trees become too large ; they are almost free of disease and, as a bonus, they are exceptionally beautiful, particularly when in bloom. The avenue is provided with park benches.

The play parks have been differentiated for various interests and purposes. The aim is to provide as many play opportunities as possible, and at the same time a place for rest and relaxation.

The development consists of three-storey detached buildings, and parking has in general been provided under the courtyards. The population for the two play parks together numbers about 9,000.

1 ball games	5 table tennis
2 tennis court	6 playground building
3 swings	7 sand area
4 pen	8 flower garden
	9 huts

1 Carts need a smooth asphalt surface
2 Model of the play park, Turkosen
3 Sand section at Turkosen
4 The central play court, Turkosen
5 Plan of the development
6 Model of Opalen play park

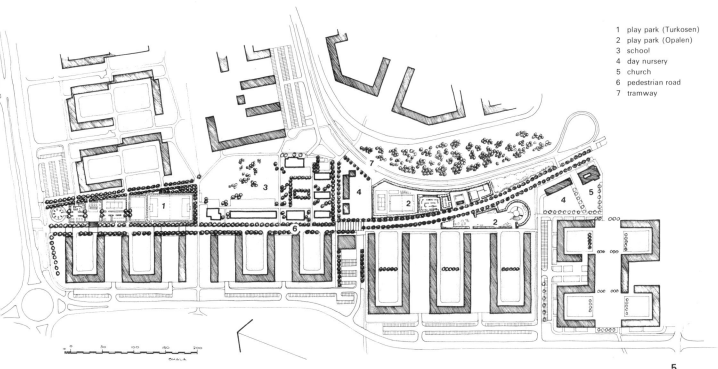

1 play park (Turkosen)
2 play park (Opalen)
3 school
4 day nursery
5 church
6 pedestrian road
7 tramway

5

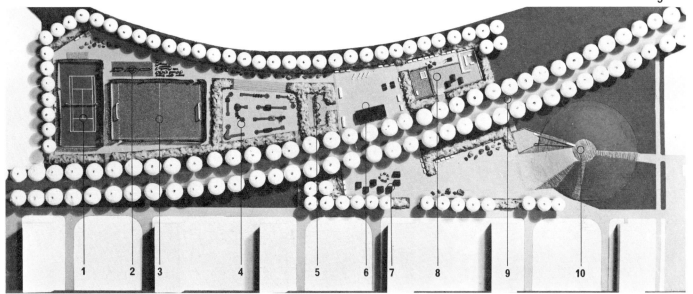

6

1 tennis
2 gymnastic equipment
3 football
4 mini golf
5 swings
6 supervised play
7 wendy houses
8 sand play
9 pedestrian path
10 hill with chute and hard track

4

125

TOPASEN

This development, which is situated in rocky and very rolling ground, has been systematically designed with vehicle-free pedestrian streets. The height of the buildings varies from three to six storeys, according to the ground. Car parking is provided, partly in parking blocks and partly under the courtyards. There are about 3,000 residents.

The play park and schools are situated in a vehicle-free central area between the housing groups. To obtain as strong a contrast as possible to the regulated and orderly living environment, it was considered appropriate that the play park should emphasize the rolling landscape and try to take advantage in the best way of its potential play opportunities. The basin-shaped rock formation in the middle section lent itself to arrangement as a series of shallow paddling pools on various levels, connected by little streams of

waterfalls. A natural rock crevice, with an adventurous atmosphere and bordered by large stone slabs, will later be used as a sand playground for the more advanced sand players. Sandplay for small children has been provided on a sunny hill face with plenty of seats for the mothers. The small cultivated sites left by the original cottage development have been utilized in various ways, among others for ball game courts, and it proved possible to squeeze in one more of these than the plan indicates. In the course of the work, certain other departures from the plan were made. The group of Wendy houses has for example been moved down to the central play piazza from the rock crest intended for it and instead a wooden floor, which is suitable as a dance floor has been placed there if young people should feel like moving to the din of transistors.

1

1 Plan of the development
2 Model of the play park
3 Water play
4 Winter play slope
5 Grouped play huts furnished with loose wooden blocks

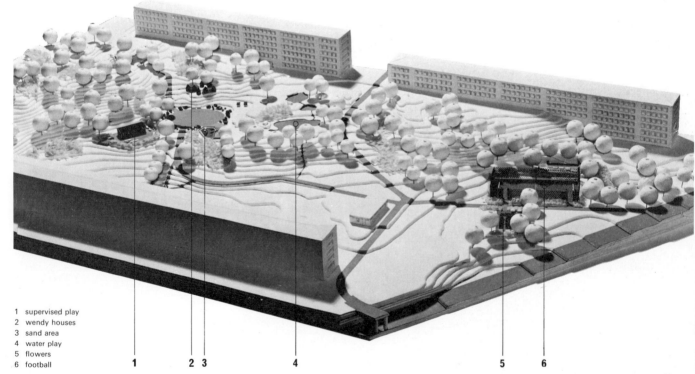

1 supervised play
2 wendy houses
3 sand area
4 water play
5 flowers
6 football

1   2 3   4   5 6

2

4

3

5

6

7

6   View from the sand area to the dance floor
    on the rock
7   The central play court

BERGKRISTALLEN

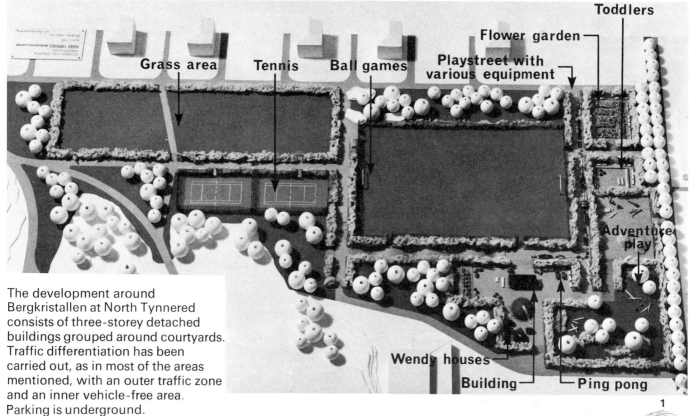

Grass area　Tennis　Ball games　Playstreet with various equipment　Flower garden　Toddlers

Wendy houses　Building　Ping pong　Adventure play

The development around Bergkristallen at North Tynnered consists of three-storey detached buildings grouped around courtyards. Traffic differentiation has been carried out, as in most of the areas mentioned, with an outer traffic zone and an inner vehicle-free area. Parking is underground.

The play park is on level ground adjacent to a wooded sector where the school and youth centre for the area has been situated. The large central playing field in the play park is consequently intended for school use, but outside of school hours it is generally available. The components of the play park are apparent from the photograph of the model. Each unit is surrounded by a six-foot high earth mound planted with willows. The play street formed between the various sections has been designed and equipped for play. In certain sections it has an undulating profile for bicycle play. Another section of the play street has been equipped with a so-called shipwreck—a series of play units so placed that the children can move some way along them without touching the ground.

It is intended to develop the large sandy section into an adventure playground when vegetation has grown sufficiently to make a suitable frame for it. The play park is still under development.

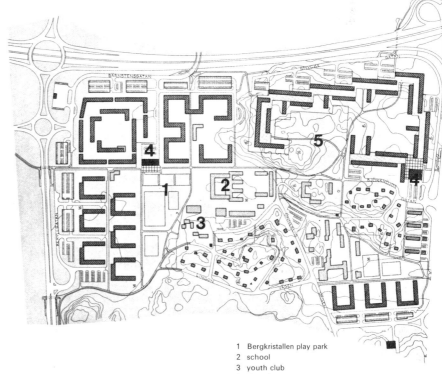

1　Model of the play park
2　Plan of the housing area

1　Bergkristallen play park
2　school
3　youth club
4　shopping
5　Spaden play park

129

POSITIVET

The surrounding housing area
is characterized by a very concentrated tower block development
peripherally situated around a large,
vehicle-free, central open area which,
in addition to recreational facilities,
also contains schools of all stages,
from nursery school to high school.
The catchment area of Positivet
amounts to about 5,000 residents.

The play park is on level ground but
is complemented by the adjacent
hilly area. The circular play area and
the playground building are
surrounded by play arrangements of
various types, mostly ball-game
courts. At present the possibility of
extending the play park by an
adventure playground is being
investigated.

1   Plan of play park
2, 3   The circular play area – on a winter
       morning and on a summer day
4   Plan of the housing area

2

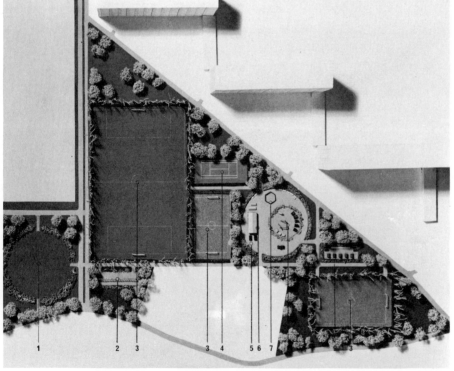

3

1   playing field
2   swings
3   ball games
4   tennis court
5   table tennis
6   indoor play house
7   infants
8   sand play
9   wendy house

1

1 play park Positivet
2 play park Slottsberget
3 high school
4 primary school
5 secondary school
6 shopping centre
7 recreation area

4

SPINNETPLATSEN

The surrounding development consists of one three-storey building about 800 metres (880 yds) long, forming the actual framework of the play park, and sixteen twelve-storey tower blocks. The total population is about 4,000.

The play park is situated on sloping ground and adjoins the primary school. The rock formations within the playing area were originally covered with vegetation; this

2

attraction. The central play court is the core of the layout and the other play arrangements are set around it. Among these are a large grass playing field, a sandpit, ball game courts and a small corner for adventure play with a sandy base. The adventure play area is not yet in use as the vegetation has not grown sufficiently to screen it from the rest of the development.

1, 2, 6   Central play court
3   Plan of the playground
4   Plan of the housing area
5, 7   The play rock
8   The old locomotive

1

however was considered unable to withstand the heavy wear a play park involves. The vegetation and loose earth were therefore removed and the rocks made into a play hill with play cabins, a slide and seats. A water pipe was led up to the crest to give possibilities for water play. The water runs in a natural crevice in the rock, and in its course it forms little pools and waterfalls. The flow of water is regulated by the play leader.

The play house with its surrounding play area is situated centrally. The surface of this part is asphalt and there are tables for table tennis, tables and benches for games and general get-togethers, car tyres in piles and stone blocks of various sizes. In the middle of all this towers an old steam engine as a gigantic sculpture which at the same time forms a popular play

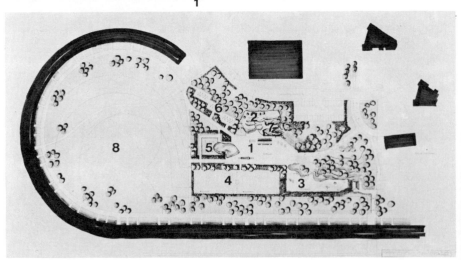

3

1	play yard with playground building	5 sand area
2	rocks	6 swings
3	adventure play	7 streamlet
4	ball games	8 playing field

6

5

7

8

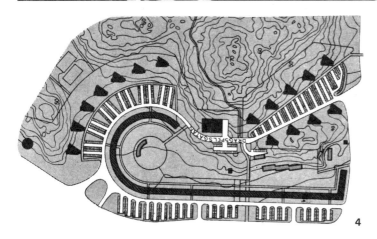

4

FLATÅS

The development consists of three- and four-storey detached buildings grouped in such a manner that they form enclosed courtyards, towards which all entrances face. Service traffic is kept outside and parking plots are situated outside the actual development. The population is about 7,000.

The play park is centrally situated within the vehicle-free sector and is adjacent to school and playing fields. Because of its situation, it has come to be used extensively as a school playground during the longer breaks.

As with the town plan, the play park is built up from separate space forms which, in the case of the play

—which is frequently considered by adults to be lacking in order of any kind. The division of the area into courtyards or spaces provides conditions for a substantially greater number of different activities than if the whole area, for example, had been laid out as one grassy surface. At the same time, protection against the wind and a more interesting play landscape has been provided.

The play park is supervised by a qualifed playleader who constantly initiates improvements which are generally carried out with the children's help. The layout shown by the plan does not, therefore, correspond in its details to the

present situation. The play cabin town for example has been moved to the central play area in front of the playground building, and in its place a meeting point for teenagers is beginning to evolve under an erected roof.

That part of the development mostly open to alteration is, of course, the adventure playground, which is in continuous development. A house—even the most interesting— is rarely allowed more than a few months' life, and the torn-down houses provide material for continuous building.

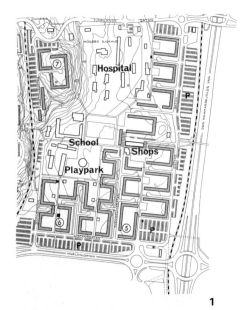

1

park, have been effected by planted earth mounds. The planting is of willow (Salix purpurea), which thrives under heavy pruning ; consequently, children can be allowed to break as many branches as they wish without damaging the vegetation more than temporarily.

The strict square plan, here illustrated by a photograph of the model, may give an impression of a far too orderly world of play. In fact, one encounters only one courtyard at a time, not the general survey given by the plan. One moves from one ''room'' to the next as if in a building. The order is often the children's own

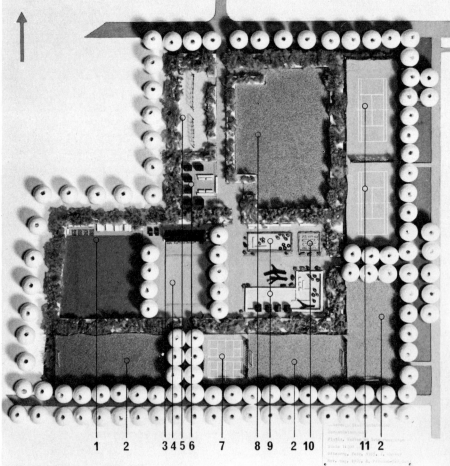

2

1 quiet corner	7 badminton courts
2 football field	8 adventure playground
3 supervised play	9 sand play
4 hard surface area	10 flowers
5 swings	11 tennis courts
6 wendy house	

5

3

6

4

1   Plan of the area
2   Model of the play park
3   Football area
4   The play park is for all ages
5   Sand play area
6   Flower garden kept by the children
    themselves

7, 8, 9, 10, 11   The adventure play area
12   Rocks and stones of various sizes
        alternate with smooth asphalt

11

12

Two play parks in Länsmansgården, Gothenburg

Landscape architects: The Park Department, Gothenburg.

The character of the landscape is that of an archipelago, with bare, weathered rocks and sparse vegetation of juniper, sloe and heather. In planning the playgrounds, we have tried as far as possible to preserve these natural assets and to make the best possible use of their play potential. The greatest difficulty was to provide suffcent flat surfaces for ball games, tennis courts, etc.

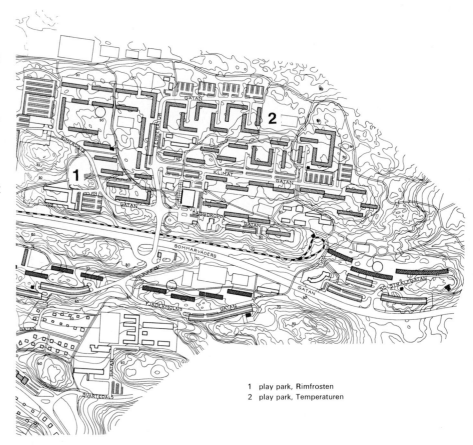

1 play park, Rimfrosten
2 play park, Temperaturen

1 RIMFROSTEN

The play park is directly connected to a primary school, and acts partly as the school courtyard. Contact with the housing area north of the play park is effected through two pedestrian tunnels under the street. The differences in ground levels has been utilized in various ways, including an asphalted track that has been provided on the hill slope. This is intended for toboggans during the winter and for carts during the summer. A slide has been provided so that one can move from one level to the other.

The central, level section is fenced with wire netting and covered with red asphalt. The surface is intended as a general play area during the summer and as a skating rink during the winter.

1 Model of the play park
2 Central asphalt area sprayed as an ice rink

1

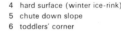

1 sleigh run
2 gymnastic equipment
3 swings
4 hard surface (winter ice-rink)
5 chute down slope
6 toddlers' corner
7 supervised play
8 wendy houses
9 sand play
10 ping pong

2

139

5

3

6

3 The playground seen against the rocky hill
4 Winter sleigh run
5 Sand play sector
6 The mounting ladder of the slide is inside
   a tunnel of tractor tyres

4

2 TEMPERATUREN

As at Rimfrosten, a flat surface has been obtained by filling out a marshy area. In this way it has been possible to complement the rocky landscape by those play arrangements which require level ground, for example ball game courts.

The central section within the play park has an asphalt surface which has been provided with, among other things, groups of natural stone and with piles of car tyres of various heights. A play mound three metres high, also covered with asphalt, is intended for play with carts and cars during the summer and as an ice slide during the winter. The cirular mound around the central sand ground is

paved with stone to withstand heavy wear. It is possible to swing by means of ropes out into the sand from the top of the mound.

Arrangements for sand play were considered to be essential in a landscape almost entirely of hard surfaces. Consequently, the play park includes two more sections for sand play, one for the younger children and their supervisors and one for somewhat more energetic sand play. The children can of course still move freely and any division into age groups, apart from that made by the parents, does not exist. The section equipped with an eye to the small children is abundantly provided with

little play corners and plenty of seating facilities for those looking after them.

For the teenagers, a meeting point has been arranged in the south-western corner of the play park. This is enclosed by long benches and furnished with fixed table-tennis tables and equipment for playing chess with large pieces. The section has, however, not yet found its final form. Youth is fastidious when choosing a place for recreation and likes to have a word in the matter of design. The area is open for the exercise of good initiative.

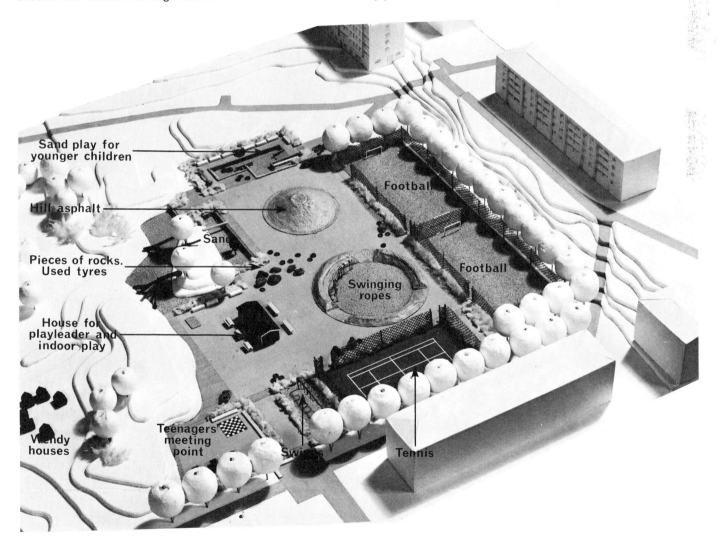

4

2

5

3

6

2 Table tennis area sheltered by a wooden
   wall
3 Work tables outside the playground building
4 The central area
5 Play hut
6 The asphalt-surfaced hill is popular for
   cycling and cart riding
7 Circular bank for rope games
8 From the top of the hill you can run your
   cart right into the sand — furthest wins

7

8

143

Orrholmen, Karlstad, Sweden

Landscape architect: Eric Anjou, FSTL.

The play park, which was provided on the initiative of the newspaper *Expressen*, is centrally situated in the Orrholmen housing estate at Karlstad. The population is about 3,000 and the play park covers an area of about 15,000 m² (4 acres).

The play unit has been grouped around a play court in such a manner that each element can be extended if necessary. A streamlet in an asphalt bed has been introduced as a boundary between the organised part of the park and the open grass area. An adventure play ground enclosed by a wooden fence can, incidentally, be observed among the elements. Towards the court, the fence has been angled to provide niches, protected from the wind for playing table tennis.

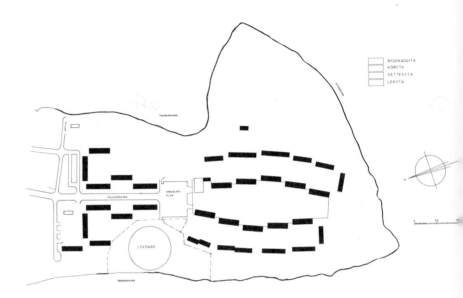

ORRHOLMEN

1

2

4

3

1 Plan of the housing estate
2 Gymnastics
3 Sand area with slides
4 The play park is the meeting place of the housing area, where parties and entertainments for everybody are arranged
5 Plan of the play park

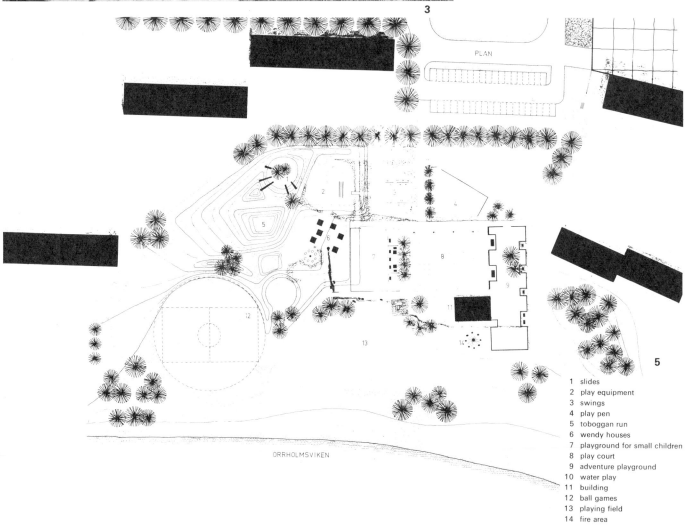

PLAN

ORRHOLMSVIKEN

5

1 slides
2 play equipment
3 swings
4 play pen
5 toboggan run
6 wendy houses
7 playground for small children
8 play court
9 adventure playground
10 water play
11 building
12 ball games
13 playing field
14 fire area

K

6

8

7

6 Sand play area
7 The pump housing for the stream has been
   designed as play equipment
8 The stream
9, 10 Adventure playground
11 Carpentry by the very young

10

9

11

Nuneaton Play Park, England

Landscape architect: Mary Mitchell, FILA.

The park differs completely from the Swedish examples so far described. The surrounding development consists mainly of detached and terraced houses, and has in general a country-like atmosphere. The park has the character of a landscape, with green fields, beautiful groups of trees and a large, bright water area for fishing and paddling.

Two enormous play mounds of excavation material from the area form a dominant feature of the park landscape. To withstand the heavy wear expected, they have been given a concrete surface by spraying a cement mixture on to a reinforcement

2

of steel wire netting. The mounds have slides, and an aerial rope-way has been provided from one mound to the other.

The large pond is a valued feature of the park and a great attraction

because of the fishing. The play park also contains a paddling pool, adjacent to the section for sand play. Toilets and a filter plant for the pond have been incorporated in the plan.

1

3

5

4

1 Aerial ropeway between two mounds
2 Paddling pool, toilets and sand area
3 Play sculpture designed by Fabio Barra-
   clough
4, 5 The lake

Playground at Expo 67, Montreal, Canada

Architect: Cornelia Hahn Oberlander, ASLA.

The playground was a part of the Creative Centre at the Canadian Federal Pavilion at the World's Fair. The area was about 38 × 18 metres (125 × 60 ft) and the objective was to offer new ideas for crowded urban communities.

Cornelia Hahn Oberlander says: "When I was asked to design the playground, I asked myself, 'What is it that children really like to do?' They like to run, to climb, to crawl, to build, to feel contrasting textures, and see colours. In creating the playground, it was my task, as designer, to interpret the ideas of an educator and to relate those to design principles in order to achieve a total environment for 'Education for Creativity'. The restful, garden-like atmosphere of gentle mounds, pine trees, and hedges is purposefully created to contrast with the concrete and asphalt jungle effect of the world of the city child."

The area had many opportunities for active and creative outlets. A sand and canal area provided several attractions. To reach the sand area, a child had to balance on logs or cross tiny, arched bridges or just leap across the water. A four-inch deep canal with flowing water wound around the sand areas.

The nursery area was separated from the rest by a four-foot cedar hedge. It comprised a sand box, water play area, rabbit cages, playhouse, climbing teepee, flower pots with a great variety of plants placed on the periphery to be watered and studied by the children. A step-seating arrangement was provided for mothers to sit with shy youngers to help them overcome any fear of strangeness.

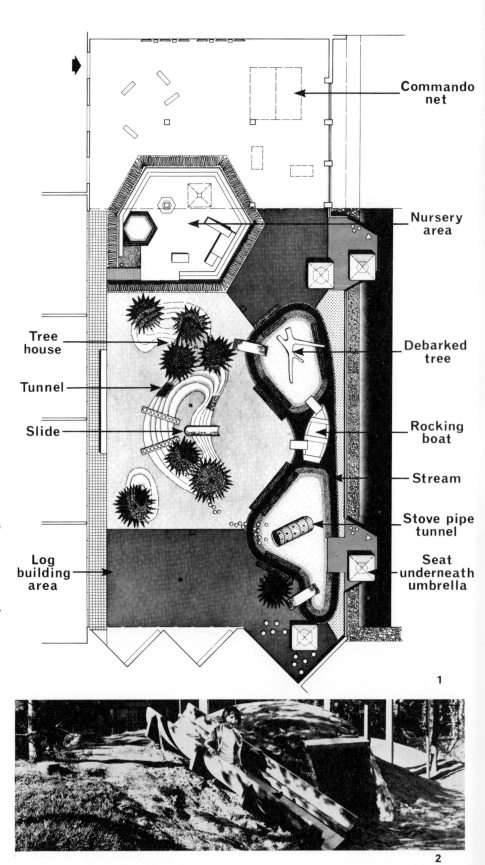

1

2

Commando net

Nursery area

Debarked tree

Rocking boat

Stream

Stove pipe tunnel

Seat underneath umbrella

Tree house

Tunnel

Slide

Log building area

3

5

4

1   Plan
2   Wooden slide and tunnel entrance
3   Playhouse with slide
4   The boat can be rocked, but not over-
    turned
5   Tree house, reached in 3 ways: rope ladder,
    wooden ladder, step ladder
6   Sketch of the playground

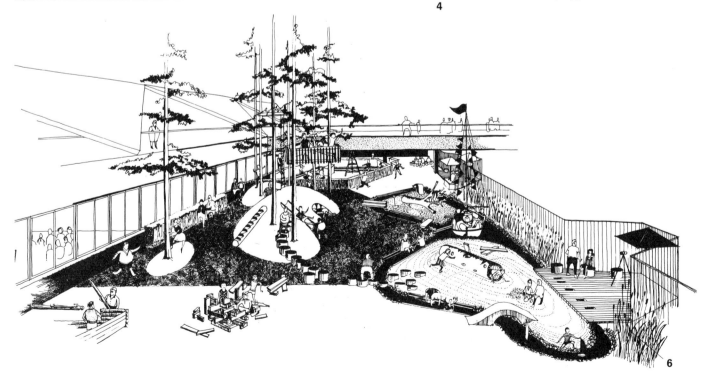

6

Mitake Children's Centre, Tokyo

Architect: Tange.
Landscape architect: Hayashi.

Simply, yet boldly conceived, and finished in exposed aggregate concrete panels, set within a carefully constructed landscape. Studios, music rooms, libraries and indoor play rooms are lively throughout the day with all age groups of children, who come and go with complete freedom, and seem remarkably well-behaved. Set individually within the general scheme are pushbutton models in well-designed show cases which demonstrate aspects of transport, industry, the postal service, and so on.

The careful modelling of the playground as part of the overall landscape design provides an area of play barely visible from the road, sheltered by the subtle shaping of the exterior bank, and softened by grass and mature trees. Hard landscaping in concrete and surfaces of tarmacadam at different levels, make for interesting contrasts of form and textures. There is, however, not a

great deal of planting, and the playground has been called too tectonic.

The principal play-sculpture is globular, has openings large enough for the children to clamber through, and is set in a hollowed-out area surfaced with sand and retained by low curved concrete walls. Sand pits and various kinds of climbing equipment are sited in sheltered pockets so that the younger children

can play in peace, undisturbed by roller-skating and the general hum and activity around them. Perhaps the most popular feature is the smooth-surfaced, bowl-shaped mound which provides endless fun for children sliding up and down the face. A short cut to the top of the mound via the slippery surface challenges the adventurous, while the more cautious may climb the sides by foothold blocks.

Text by Kuro Kaneko and Mary Mitchell

THE COMPONENTS OF THE PLAYGROUND

The outdoor room

Far too often we talk as though creating a playground was a matter of equipment alone, a matter of providing the right play-tools and satisfactory playthings, but more important than anything else is the playground itself, the place where the activities will take place. What is it like? Will the proportions create a feeling of security and intimacy? Is it a pleasant environment? Is there shelter from wind? Will it be too hot in the sun? These questions—and there are certainly others—are seldom asked.

Everyone has strong views on the subject of interiors, having experienced draught and discomfort, but we seldom try to analyze the qualities of an area which is out-of-doors. Generally speaking the same rules apply in both instances, even if material and style do not necessarily coincide. When working with greenery, for instance, right angles need not necessarily be the most suitable. Freedom is unlimited and perhaps that is the difficulty. In favourable circumstances the layout of the surrounding buildings may create harmonious spaces between them, but massive blocks too often create vast spaces which have little in common with human proportions or with their proper function. Such areas must be subdivided and carefully differentiated so that they can all become useful.

One of the most common reasons for our failure with regard to playgrounds is that we overlook the need for some sort of enclosing wall or screen which will bring a room-like quality. Playgrounds are often far too open, windy and disagreeable. We are too concerned that every corner should be in full view, and this can make children go and play somewhere else. They hide away in cellars and lofts, in garages and bicycle-sheds, and of course in the shrubbery on the housing estate, which is often the only 'playground' offering a bit of privacy. Must we really know everything, see everything and control everything in a child's life? Nobody imposes

1

anything like the same interference on the country child. They have haystacks, barns, woodlands and so on, and no-one sees anything dangerous to society in that. Conditions in towns are certainly different and the risks greater in many respects, but our fears and precautions can also become oppressive, and have a totally unintended effect.

It is essential to create a room-like atmosphere in most areas of play; the sandpit is nothing but a sad area of sand if there are no walls of some kind. One must not forget, however, that the "room" is seen from the eye-level of a sitting child, and that high walls are not needed for the desired effect to be achieved in a sandpit. Enclosures can be devised in many ways—from ramparts, plantings, planks, bricks, etc. Anything capable of use as a hiding-place can be desirable from a child's point of view. As children, we have all discovered the cosy "room" under a well-draped table, where the table-cloth almost reaches the floor. The

child's fantasy seems to flourish best when the adult world is completely shut out.

Playground surfaces are of great importance. We need soft sand surfaces with generous measurements, repeated as often as feasible;

2

4

3

involve bicycles, pushcarts and toy cars. Incidentally, who said that all surfaces should be level? An undulating asphalt surface is often far more interesting than a level one, and why not break the monotony with a few large boulders? In all their simplicity they manage to spur the imagination on the most varied adventures. At one time they are watch towers, at another boats on a vast ocean. Sometimes they support a fantastic construction of bricks and bits of wood, sometimes they are faithful playmates with human names and the great advantage of always being there. Tree trunks of various shapes and sizes are welcome additions since they, too, will animate an otherwise dull surface.

1 Small spaces inside a bigger one. Stuttgart, W. Germany
2 The floor is an important part of every room
3 Long grass and small children – just sit down and you are in a world of your own
4 A room-like quality can be achieved in many ways. Dell playground, Birmingham

we need grassy surfaces which are agreeable to move on and far too valuable to be fenced off. What may be less obvious is that we also need hard smooth surfaces. Why should we turn our noses up at asphalt? It is monotonously dull to the more sophisticated eye of an adult, but children certainly do not despise it at an age when most of their games

Loose material

Many playgrounds are most popular while they are under construction, when there are still bits of wood and mounds of earth all over the place. When it is finally finished, the children's interest often wanes. The playing equipment is soon explored, and planned play activities are a diminishing enticement if the possibilities of variation are limited.

What is most often lacking in playgrounds and in our housing estates in general, is loose material which will serve the child's inventive and creative drive. Everything is normally so finished, so well-arranged that nothing is left to the child's initiative. This is a mistake; children want a part in creating their own play world, but the opportunities are few in the average modern residential estate. It is not surprising that play often becomes destructive instead of constructive.

Photo: Gunvor Persson

2

1

3

1 A modern housing area is generally so well kept and tidy that children can find practically nothing in the way of constructional material
2 Many playgrounds are at their most active while under construction
3 Fixed equipment alone never makes a real playground

156

Adventure play

Everyone brought up in the country will have built huts of branches or sticks, farmyards of stones, pirates' caves in rock crevices and other kinds of constructions long since forgotten. Perhaps most town children, too, have at one time or another known the pleasure of building, even if in secret and with an uneasy conscience. Adventure play has always existed, even in town. Children hide in park bushes and perhaps dig themselves an underground cave hidden from passers-by. Or they will dare anything and fix a platform high up in a tree ! They work almost day and night, well knowing that they may be stopped at any time. The house sways wildly in the wind, and passers-by shake their heads at the "youth of today". Then someone rings the police or the park superintendent, and the fun is over for the time being.

But surely it is not impossible, even in town, to legitimize this urge of children to build and create their own play-environment, without endangering the "law and order" that we adults so uncompromisingly demand ? In our adult system we will have to set aside small reserves in which the children's own law and order is allowed to prevail. The answer to this need is the adventure playground that today has left its experimental stage. Adventure playgrounds now exist in most Western countries. It is true that they are not always successful, but this is far from the rule, and the failures are often due to half-hearted enterprise. Adventure play has often been preached as a "doctrine of salvation" ; it has involved a radical conversion and a break with the past, and many sceptics have been forced, more or less against their will, to provide experimental playgrounds. It is not surprising, perhaps, if these were not always successful.

It would be wrong to suppose that adventure playgrounds have made other kinds of playgrounds superfluous ! This is certainly not the case. The adventure playground is a very valuable complement of the

Photo: Gunvor Persson

general concept of playgrounds, a section among others, just as natural and in no way more exclusive. What is required is a suitable area, linked in a natural way to the general layout of the housing area. To try to hide it in some back area is to fail from the outset. It will almost certainly become a "hide out" and probably not a desirable one.

How large should an adventure playground be ?
The area can vary according to circumstances. As a component in a well-differentiated play park, 1500 sq. metres ($\frac{1}{3}$ acre) might be sufficient, since play is spread among the various other sections. If all play is to take place within the adventure playground considerably more space is needed, perhaps 10,000 sq. metres ($2\frac{1}{2}$ acres). This large area should then be divided into smaller units for wind protection and to give a more concentrated environment. Children have a great sense of atmosphere, even if at times we may be tempted to believe the opposite. Given the opportunity to choose, they almost always choose the intimacy of the small—indeed, quite often very small—space. In fact crowding appears to be an additional attraction.

The space division of an area can be arranged in various ways. A planted earth bank has many advantages and gives an immediate

effect which will be further improved as the vegetation develops. However, it requires space and can only be used in the case of the larger concepts. For small areas, a wall or wooden fence is the best solution.

What type of ground ?
All are suitable provided they are not so hard that it is impossible, for example, to insert a corner post for a

3

5

4

6

hut, and not so poorly drained that it is unsuitable for play during a rainy period. Drainage is important and it may even be necessary to replace the top-soil layer with gravel.

The material for building
Although the demand for building material is high, almost anything can be used. Empty wooden boxes are very useful as they create a lot of

1, 2 *To country children an adventure play-ground offers nothing new — it is their normal way of playing*
3 *Building a house*
4 *A notice board tells what is going on*
5 *An adventure playground is not just construction. It is also having a good time*
6 *House building is for girls too, particularly the home-making side of it*

159

activity and can sometimes serve as a complete room. Timber of various lengths, old car tyres, bricks, cardboard boxes, old furniture, rolls of wallpaper, bits of rope, paint etc. The list is unending, since most things are welcome. The main point is to adapt the supply of material as much as possible to the need. Extensive stocks are not essential, but on the other hand the supply should not run out for any length of time as activities are soon affected. It is best to obtain "suppliers"—factories, shops, etc.—

from whom a regular supply of waste material can be collected.

Tools, nails etc
All tools must be of good quality. Toy tools are not recommended : they do not last and they make difficult work harder. Knocking in nails with a real hammer is difficult enough. Hammers, saws and pliers are the tools most needed, and should be present in sufficent numbers to prevent interruption of activities. Nails must sometimes be rationed in accordance with the supply.

7　The house may go on growing all summer
8　Destruction is no less important than construction and prevents the playground from becoming static
9　A place should be set aside for a store of materials
10　Spring cleaning
11–17　Good tools are essential

8

7

10

11

12

Photo: Elnar Liljequist   13

Photo: Stig Billing   15

14

16

17

L

19

Fencing
All building sites present a disorderly and untidy appearance, and it would be too much to ask that the children's should be an exception. To expect rigorous orders or high aesthetic values would scarcely be consistent with the throw-out building material or the creative play we strive for. In fact, on an adventure playground the finished construction is of little interest. It is the period of creation

which is all-important, and as long as the creative urge is maintained a building is under continual development. The small, insignificant hut may be extended until it becomes a creation of several floors, verandas and balconies, with an interior which might best be described as labyrinthine.

To incorporate all this activity in a polished and ready-formed town environment, an outside frame is

20

18   Gardening area
19   Site clearing in progress
20   The corner posts have to be well founded
21, 23   Music gives atmosphere
22   Handing out tools
24   The leader – more important than anything else on the playground

18

21

23

22

24

necessary to prevent the "disorder" from overflowing and, at the same time keep people from looking in. The frame is valuable from the child's point of view as it prevents the adult world from penetrating too much and so provides a sheltered play environment. Professor C. Th. Sørensen had a massive, planted, earth mound erected around his classic "junk playground" outside Copenhagen which now encompasses everything with its greenery. Notting Hill Adventure Playground in London (Lady Allen of Hurtwood), which may well become a classic, is enclosed by a high wall. In other places, wooden fences and palisades have been successfully used. Indeed, even industrial fencing is acceptable if it is complemented with greenery.

The fencing serves as a shelter and a space-creator, but it has another task, as a barrier. It is necessary, generally, to have fixed opening times and, to prevent damage, etc, it may be advisable to lock the entrance at other times.

The play leader
The most important factor of an adventure playground is no doubt the play leader. Indeed, an adventure playground without a suitable leader is nothing more than a space filled with rubbish, and constructive activity soon stops. This very question of the leader is perhaps the most difficult nut to crack, because there is no professional group with suitable training. When only an isolated adventure playground is concerned, it is usually possible to hand-pick some naturally gifted person for the job; but if we accept adventure playgrounds on a wider basis, the question of training must be solved.

EVEN THE TRADITIONAL PLAYGROUND CAN BE BROUGHT ALIVE

What is needed is construction material and some sort of basic structures. Wooden blocks in great numbers are used in many Swedish playgrounds.

1

1, 2, 3   Frame for construction designed by Robert Montan

2

3

6

5

7

*4, 5, 6, 7, 8   Nola huts, designed by Olof Nola,
in the playground at Slottskogen, Gothenburg*

4

8

165

Fire

It is important for modern children to learn what fire is. This is not usually achieved as a matter of course, since there are few open fireplaces where the child can learn, under supervision, about fire and what it is.

There should be a fire playground in an adventure playground. The material used for building usually burns quite easily, and if anybody in a child-built hut should start experimenting with fire accidents can easily happen. In such an event it is possible to imagine the entire adventure playground going up in flames.

The fire playground can be arranged in various ways. One, found in Danish adventure playgrounds, is to have a fire burning continuously. The children playing with the fire take brands from the large fire to smaller fires placed in a circle around the large fire. At the small fires the children can then play with fire by igniting various materials and finding out how well or how badly they burn. It often happens that a child, coming to such an adventure playground for the first time, spends a great deal of the first week on the fire playground. Only after this does he start building. This—if it happens in the right way— is just as it should be. If children have a thorough knowledge of fire, acquired for themselves through various tests and experiments, they will take care to avoid being careless with fire in the houses they build themselves.

Fire can also be provided in an old barrel or the like. It is not as good, but from a safety point of view the old barrel can have its advantages.

Text by Nic Nilsson

1

2

1 *Emderup adventure playground, Copenhagen*
2 *Flatås, Gothenburg*
3 *Zürich, Switzerland*

3

Live animals

Materially speaking, animals have ceased to play an essential part in town life, but there is not doubt that, for emotional reasons, they must still retain a place in it. There are children whose constant dream it is to own an animal, of any kind, so long as they can feed and pet it. This does not necessarily mean that they are capable of looking after an animal, but the need to inspire and give affection is unmistakably present, and we have every reason to foster and satisfy this urge.

But are animals in playgrounds realistic? There are undoubtedly many practical objections: financial, sanitary, administrative and other problems enter into the picture and must be considered, but they are not insoluble! A keeper travelling round a town's playgrounds to look after animals should cause no more administrative difficulties than a gardener who looks after the flowers. Problems of hygiene could be overcome by ensuring thorough cleanliness. The financial expense could hardly amount to anything prohibitive since only ordinary domestic animals, cheap to procure and easy to look after, would be involved. Rabbits, sheep, goats and other tame animals, which do not mind being stroked and which eat often and willingly, are more suitable than exotic animals kept behind bars.

If a playground is to be equipped with animals, a fundamental condition must be that their well-being is guaranteed, that children are not allowed to be too rough, and that the animals have time for resting. According to the experiments made in various playgrounds, this does not seem to pose any great problem. The animals gradually merge into their environment and become an

1

accepted part of the playground scene, but it should not be assumed that their upkeep is to be left entirely to the children. There are of course many children who would be only too happy to take on the task, but supervision is still essential.

1 Children's Zoo, London
2 At a playground in Helsingborg
3 In London, mobile zoos pay visits to parks and playgrounds
4 The children's own rabbit cages at a playground in Copenhagen
5 The marvel of hatching eggs

Acting

Acting is a common form of game. The favourite parts are those of father, mother and child. Usually it is events that have made a deep impression on a child's experience which are acted out in one form or another. A visit to the hospital or denist, a funeral in the family, etc, can provide inspiration for such games for weeks after the event and they often crop up from time to time over the years. The roles played are many and varied, and the dialogue develops during the action.

Such acting is not always performed before an audience, in fact attention from outsiders can spoil concentration and imagination. On the other hand a public is sometimes the main incentive. "Watch how clever I am!" "See, how funny I look!" It is, above all, this latter form of acting that I would like briefly to discuss. Without doubt this kind of acting is an expression of a strong need common to many children and I think we should do our utmost to fulfil this need. I believe that this form of creativity is especially important for the withdrawn child. The character assumed in a play will be brave and can do all those things which one would not dare to do oneself. We can safely say things when playing the part of a teacher, policeman or crook, which we would not dare to say as ourselves.

Costumes are often not needed, but it is always a great help to dress up, however simple. A costume, even a rag round the head, makes a child bolder and a clothes-chest is therefore an important piece of equipment in a playground. The contents can often be collected by the children themselves. Almost anything is useful : an old slip and some old curtains make a wonderful wedding dress, a pair of outsized shoes can be wildly funny, and so on.

The stage can be a doorway, a small verandah or just a slight elevation in the ground. Often, following the principles of modern theatre, the play is acted in the middle of the "room", but a stage, even of the simplest kind, and some means of

2

1

hanging a curtain would help. The curtain can be a couple of old sheets or blankets, but they should be capable of being drawn. In a playground with an imaginative playleader this can always be arranged in one way or another, but why not make everything easier by having a simple, standard fixture in the playground's equipment, preferably one which permits other uses ? A small platform about 0·5 m (1 ft 6 in) high can be used for several purposes, especially if made of boards so that the children can dance there as well. Children love to move in time to music, and there seems to be a greater interest in music among youth today than ever before.

3

1, 2, 3   Acting can be anywhere – with or
    without an audience
4   Acting in a Stockholm playground

170

Photo: Gösta Glase

4

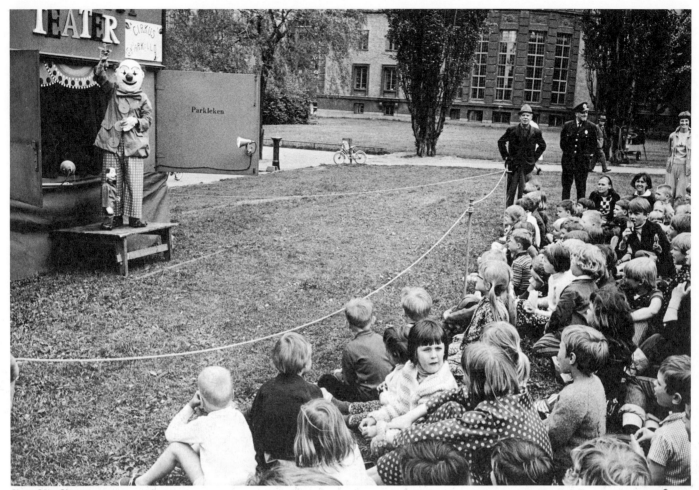

Photo: Gösta Glase

6

Photo: Erich Meler

5

7

5   Punch and Judy, Gothenburg
6   At a playground in Stockholm
7, 8   The Queen of Sheba in all her glory

8

Play Leadership

The playground is as much an element of town planning as streets and squares, and it should function at all times, more or less round the clock, even when there is no personnel. It is, however, only when personnel are present—so long as they are of the right sort—that a playground assumes its true identity.

A child needs someone to approach in critical situations, someone to talk to when everyone else is "silly", someone to ensure that the bully will not always get his way. As our towns become more impersonal, people more lonely, and as children without identity take to hanging about in doorways, so the importance of human concern and effort in our outdoor life increases, especially in relation to playgrounds.

When a playground is provided with personnel there is greater scope for equipping and developing it in an appropriate manner. Loose material can be used to a greater extent where there are personnel, and it is only then that a child really gets a chance to display its own initiative. In order to create, something to create from is needed, and it is here that the shortcomings of play life in a town are most evident. Too much is tidy and ready-made, therefore loose material from which the child can make things up must be made available.

Play must always be the first consideration when dealing with playgrounds. Organization is all right but only as a means, never as an end. A playground should never be like school, where the child is taught, and it is very important that personnel understand this, otherwise they may do more harm than good. A playground must have a free and easy atmosphere and it is vital that the personnel chosen are appropriate. Pedantic and methodical people are appropriate in many jobs in our society, but not in a playground.

Training
For one or two playgrounds, personnel can be hand-picked and

chosen as convenient, but when dealing with a comprehensive system of playgrounds it is essential to have a training scheme of some kind. However, the need for training should not be exaggerated. In the first place the right people must be chosen, those who have the ability to handle and mix with children. When making selection for training, a test for this ability is far more important than good school qualifications. In almost 20 years as a superintendent I have been able to try out play

personnel from backgrounds of practically every kind. One of the best was a middle-aged housewife with no other training than that acquired with her own children. Probably, she would have been even better, or at least have had an easier time during the first years, if she had had a certain amount of training.

The objectives of the training decide its worth. A playleader's work is entirely different from that of a school or kindergarten teacher's, and the change to playleadership for such people is often difficult. Personally, I do not believe that a playleader's training needs to be either long or very comprehensive. Practical experience is more important and it enables full advantage to be gained from the training.

Conditions of payment
Conditions of payment for play personnel are a deciding factor in the practical side of the work. Their job is more demanding than in most other work with children. They have to handle children of all ages, even teenagers, and there must be as much freedom as possible for everyone.

Consequently personnel should possess special natural qualities, not least because of the complex

situations they will have to cope with. In other words, those same people who are so much in demand for many positions in the community, and who are the object of competition. It is therefore important that we compete for them with comparable salaries.

Should the playleader be a man or a woman?
The only advantage in having a man as playleader is that during the daytime our dormitory towns consist almost entirely of women, children and the aged. A man is the exception, and this is why he is needed. The happiest solution, however, is the playground with a combination of male and female personnel. The

leadership itself will be in the hands of the most suitable person independent of the sex.

All year round occupation
Play personnel are needed all the year round, but are perhaps most necessary during the winter, when the weather makes play so unpleasant out of doors. What is there to tempt children outside when there is neither snow nor ice and it is cold and wet? During such periods personnel are needed in the playground more than ever. Equally important, if it is to be accepted as a reliable playcentre, it must be a place of regular activity. The child should accept it as a normal part of its surroundings, in the same way as the shops, for instance. A playground which only functions from time to time will never be taken seriously.

3

1–4 *A staffed playground allows far greater scope for appropriate equipment and development*

4

Indoor play

In a supervised play park, some kind of building is necessary. Toilets are desirable on all larger playgrounds, and when staff are present they are essential. Space for storing play material is also necessary, and what is to be done on rainy days or in the winter? When the rain comes down in sheets one must either move indoors to play or stop playing and go home. On cold winter days outdoor play should interchange with indoor play, since neither children nor staff will enjoy being out of doors all the time.

The building can be quite simple. It must be designed for vigorous play and take rough treatment. Fragile furniture or finishes, do not belong. It is the children's own house, and should be suited to what they themselves consider essential. And don't forget that the roof space seems to have a special attraction! More often than not it is the favourite gathering place and it can be difficult to keep the children from it. Why not design the house so that the roof space is suitable for use? The fewer taboos, the less the conflicts and the better the playground!

Photo: Einar Liljequist

2

Photo: Einar Liljequist

1

Photo: Einar Liljequist

3

5

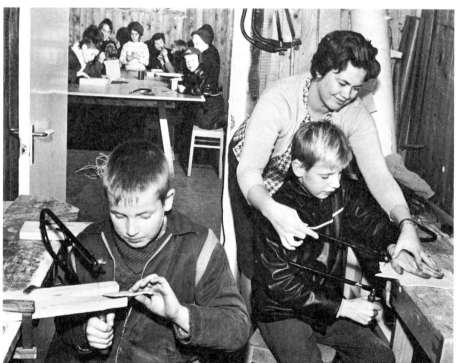

Photo: Jan Rietz

4

Building at Notting Hill Adventure Playground

Architects: Michell and Partners, London.

Materials
The permanent structure is of brick and blocks of concrete, all strongly built.

The playroom
The playroom is the largest room measuring 6 × 9 m (20 × 30 ft) and is for games, meetings and dancing, table tennis and billiards. The ceiling tiles provide heat insulation and sound absorption. A small kitchen enables the girls to do some cooking and snacks can be served through the hatch.

The activities room
This room is linked to the playroom by a lobby lined with cupboards, and is for quieter and more sedentary activities such as painting, clay modeling and crafts.

It is particularly suitable for the daytime playgroups of children under five. It has a door to the under-fives play area and a large store.

The warden's room
When he is in his room the warden occupies a key position on the plan. The door is immediately opposite the main entrance door, and when both the doors are open there is a direct view of the playground entrance gate. The room has a wide window commanding the adventure play area and a side window from which the slide, the roof ladder and the ball game area can be seen.

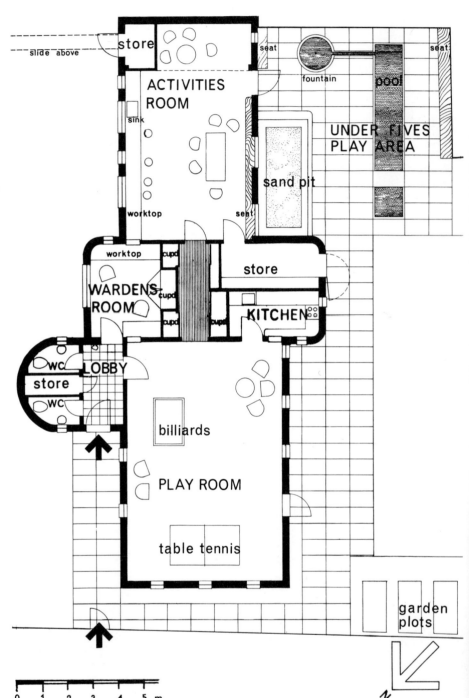

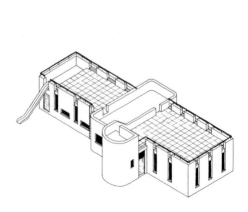

The roof
This is part of the playground and has been planned with areas for play on different levels, one of which is a turret. The roof is intended for the older children and can be reached only by climbing a steep ladder.

Building for play parks in Gothenburg

Architect: WAAB White AB.
All parts are erected on 1·2 m (4 ft) modules of wooden construction, with both outside and inside facings of wood.

The small basic unit contains a play room, store room and two toilets. A larger play room can be attached to this, or combined with one or more additional rooms. The various units can also be erected individually or joined together to form villages.

The type employed until now at Gothenburg is a stretch of 13 modules of 1·2 m, that is to say with a length of 15·6 m (52 ft). The play room has dimensions of 5 × 7 m (16 ft 6 in × 23 ft). A smaller room intended as an office for the warden is joined to this.

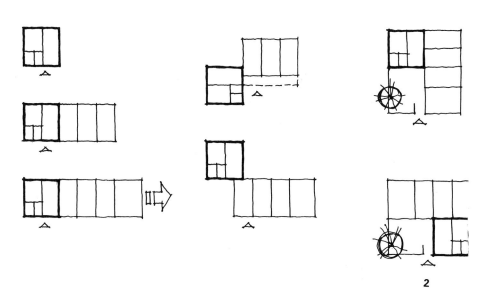

2

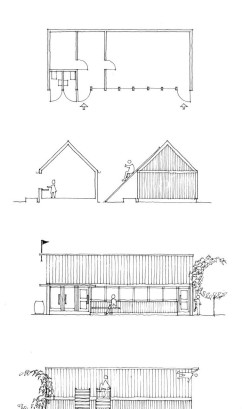

1

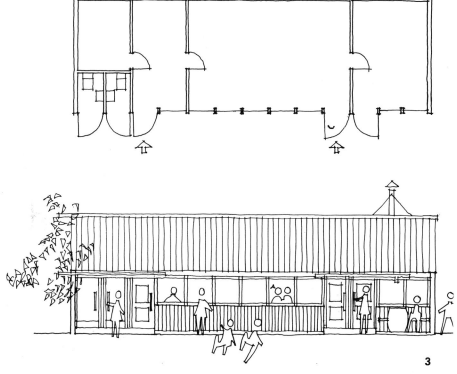

3

1 10 modules
2 The units can be joined in various ways
3 13 modules

Sand Play

Everyone enjoys playing with soft and splendid sand, building castles, digging tunnels, baking cakes or whatever takes one's fancy. Sand can be moulded into almost anything one wishes, and in this lies its great value as a play material. It is one of the few constructional materials that can easily be made available in an ordinary playground. Why then this parsimony? Why these small sandpits we so often see, where children crowd around a little heap of sand, when a large sand-covered area with several heaps of sand offers far richer opportunities for play? Why save on the best we can offer when the choice of really good alternative play material is so limited!

But what about dogs and cats? This is the usual comment when sandpits are discussed. To this, I can only say that the risk of the child encountering animal excrement during play is equally inconvenient whether we have sand areas or not. As long as children and animals use the same area, suitable fencing is the only remedy.

Be lavish with sand by all means, but lavish it with sense. Large open areas easily come to look boring if they are not divided into sections that accord with the child's own scale. This can be done with suitable protective screens, which need not be very high to give the child a feeling of seclusion and intimacy. Furnishing the area with suitable toys can also contribute to this effect.

2

3

1

Where ground conditions do not allow the water to run away naturally, draining the sand area is important. In clayey ground, the pit excavated for a sand playground is like a well, and the water must be led away. The child itself has no objection to a sand area that is like a paddling pool during wet periods. Quite the contrary! The water immediately gives the area new possibilities for play: it can be channelled into endless canals, formed into lakes and even small waterfalls, but mothers decidedly do not approve of this kind of play, particularly during the colder weather.

1   The beach as a playground
2, 4   Sand lends itself to almost anything
3   Pen for the toddlers in the large sand area
5   Children prefer nooks and corners — concrete elements give almost unlimited scope for variation

4

5

8

6

7

9

12

10

11

6   Sand play in Helsingborg
7   Sand play in Gothenburg
8, 12   Sand play area, Stuttgart
9   Sand play at Raynor Park, Sunnyvale, California
10   Sand play in Karlstad
11   Sand and water at a playground in Tokyo

183

Water Play

Children love water play in whatever form available. Puddles of water after rain have always been attractive, and water that can be channelled and extended into "lakes", waterfalls, etc, is a godsend which children know how to appreciate. Unfortunately, mothers are not always equally carried away by this phenomenon, and in the well-ordered housing estate puddles become daily less available. The rainwater is drained directly to the gutter; holes which might provide puddles are filled in; open areas are carefully drained. In other words, the world of adults expands its dominion, supremely, while the child's play environment becomes impoverished.

What possibilities are there within planned playgrounds for bringing back water for play? There is certainly no lack of them. Few materials are more rewarding for a playground-planner to work with, but usually it is cost which decides the matter. Planned water play is not usually cheap, either in installation or operation. Of course one might ask what is expensive and what is cheap when speaking of such a highly fundamental play material, but the question is not easy to answer, since it is difficult to convert play into money. Are we perhaps too ambitious? A spray, a water hose, a few small basins to splash in; these are some alternatives which can be provided without great expense.

1

2

5

3

6

4

1 Stream in an asphalt bed, Orrholmen, Sweden
2 Stream at Serra Park, Sunnyvale, California
3 At a playpark in Gothenburg, Sweden.
   When the playleader turns on the water the
   stream finds its own way down the rock, to
   the enchantment of the children
4 The paddling pool serves for play, even
   without water
5 Water play at Weissenberg, Stuttgart, W.
   Germany
6 Splashing pool at West 81 St playground,
   Central Park, New York

8

9

8   Zürich, Switzerland. Small pools at
    different levels within a larger pool
9   Baronbackarna, Sweden
10 Cheap and simple basins for water play at
    a play park in London
11 Combined paddling pool and sandpit at
    Heiligenfeld in Zürich
    The basins are set at different levels – from
    the central fountain head the water runs
    into the highest basin, thence from one
    basin to another, ending eventually in the
    sandpit
12 The fascination of running water
13 Water is great fun – even with simple
    equipment

10

11

13

Photo: John Brookes **12**

Street Play

The street has always been the natural playground for a town child, and it was not until the dominance of motor vehicles that it became transformed into a traffic preserve, exclusively. Street play, however, is with us as much as ever, even if the "playgrounds" are nothing less than a danger to life. For lack of something better, children will still play in the street or car park. Among toys, the vehicle dominates to a greater extent than ever before, and they need a level surface. If the surface of the street is more suitable for this kind of play than the playing areas, it is easy to see where the child will be. Asphalt and concrete surfaces are hard and not generally popular with parents, but they are as necessary in a playground as are the softer surfaces. A good playground should have both.

3

1 Even the slightest slope is appreciated. Gothenburg
2 Concrete slope at Tsukishima, Dai Ni, Tokyo
3, 5, 6 Wheeled toys dominate more than ever before
4 Stilts, Gothenburg
7 A hard-surfaced slope on a playground in Gothenburg is constantly in use, summer and winter

1

2

4

7

5

6

Bicycle Games

Today the bicycle is in many ways more of a toy than a means of transport. It may even be the teenagers' favourite toy and it is certainly the most accident prone, all the more so when motorized as a moped. Bicycles and mopeds are a big problem, as traffic and as playthings. What is their proper place, and where should they be allowed? If special bicycle paths are laid out in the pedestrian area of the housing estate they can easily conflict with the younger childrens' play stretches and are therefore potentially dangerous, especially as both parties are playing children, and the speed of the bicycles can be considerable. Mopeds create an additional problem: they are difficult to separate from ordinary bicycle traffic, and are far too dangerous to be allowed in an area where small children are at play.

Younger children, the under-eights for instance, could very well be allowed to ride their bicycles on normal park paths and sometimes even in the playgrounds without causing much trouble, because to let them loose in fast traffic is far too risky. The first concern must be to encourage them to learn to ride and control a bicycle well.

Teenagers and older children ride their bicycles much faster and may be classified as traffic, but they should still be kept away from motor traffic in the streets. In a segregated traffic system, however, they belong on the motor traffic side, but they should be restricted to bicycle paths

2

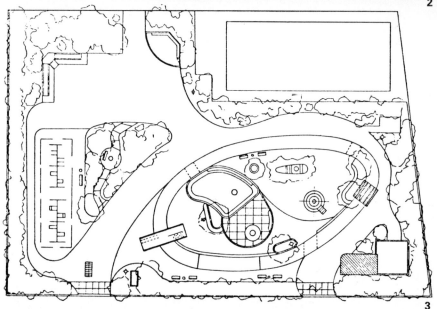

3

which run alongside the local streets, preferably separated from them by a planted verge.

Bicycle and moped playgrounds
There is a considerable demand for specially planned areas to cater for

more advanced bicycle games. Ideally, they should be linked to the network of bicycle paths, and should not be too close to housing areas, since mopeds are inevitably noisy. If surplus materials are available, a soundproofing bank could be erected around the layout, thereby making it easier to fit into the town as a whole. An indication of the lines to be followed in planning may be gained from a study of the places for such games chosen by the children themselves.

Bicycle playgrounds can even be oval-shaped like a velodrome where cyclists take it in turns to ride round a laid out track. Since speeds can be considerable, it is important for safety that the surface be banked.

1

7

5

8

6

4

1, 4, 8   Not just a means of transport
2, 3   Bicycle course at Kinryu children's play-
       ground, Tokyo
5   A mound of surplus earth adopted by the
    children for cycle games
6   "Saucer" for rollerskating and cycling at
    Triya-minami, Tokyo
7   Hill with a coating of asphalt at Tempera-
    turen play park, Gothenburg

I Dare You!

Climbing a hill, climbing a tree, climbing up on to a big rock, reaching new heights, exploring new worlds, daring more than the others, daring to do more than one thought one could do. These are activities and ambitions inseparable from children's play, and they are certainly of considerable importance in the development of personality. Risk is a stimulus, and should be present in some form even in the playground; otherwise the child chooses somewhere else for its play and for taking risks—places which are perhaps truly risky! Dare you to run across the street in front of the bus! How long do you dare to stand still before the car comes! You daren't but I dare, etc.

Whatever we may believe, children are cautious in their play so long as they can survey the situation and the consequences. A child climbing a tree rarely falls unless it climbs out onto too thin a branch. In a playground, it is often the simple well-known pursuits, when the tempo becomes high and caution is minimal, which are most accident-prone. The seemingly risky moments are often less dangerous than they seem. It is therefore important that those responsible should exercise discretion before yielding to over cautious parents, but it is of course necessary to keep constructions and fixtures under constant supervision, since failure in this respect can have catastrophic consequences.

Small children become big children little by little, and play progresses year by year. We must ensure that the

1

older children also have a place, and that their urge to play develops naturally. In these days they are often unfairly treated. All attention is concentrated on small children. As a superintendent of parks I often encounter this problem, since general opinion wishes to banish from a

playground almost everything the older children approve of, and as soon as they have found a place where they are happy and can gather together, it is referred to as a "haunt". Isn't it precisely haunts that we should strive for?

1 Play park in Helsingborg
2 Play park in London

2

Ball Games—Sports—Athletics

Special sports grounds are needed for advanced competitive games, but play and games are, by their nature, so closely related, that as a rule they simply cannot be separated. The competitive spirit is always present, even if the planners have not realized it. "I can jump like this and as far as this, how far can you jump?" Somebody kicks a football and before long a game is in full swing. The game is taken up on the spot if the sports ground is too far away, and it requires a strong will to stop it, however harmful it might be to the surroundings.

Ball game areas are thus important, and it is usually better to have many small grounds rather than one large one. Both children and adults would naturally rather play on grass if there is a choice, but in a play park for instance, which should preferably be situated not more than 300 m (350 yd) from home, grass may be a luxury. We must often make do, therefore, with some sort of hard surface. If each area is fenced in with 3 m (10 ft) high wire netting, an area of 25 × 40 m (30 × 50 yd) would be sufficient and can be surrounded with greenery, which would soon be worn out without the netting to protect it. In order to prevent accidents during play it is essential for fences to have the posts on the outside. It is also a good thing to have small openings at strategic intervals in the netting, for fetching balls which land outside, otherwise, the natural inclination might be to climb over rather than go the long way round.

In Scandinavia, Association Football is the main ball game, but the Anglo-Saxon countries have a considerably larger repertoire, and when planning play one should start with the local games, and at the same time try to introduce new ones. In recent years, for example, I have devoted myself to popularising tennis, and tennis courts are now a part of the standard equipment of a

1

2

normal play park in Gothenburg. They are simple asphalt courts, with permanent nets of steel wire, always ready for games and available without payment or advance booking. You play when the court is free or wait your turn. The disadvantage of booking in a play park community is that the courts would always be fully booked and a large group of children and adolescents who do not plan their day would never get a chance of a game. In principle, children and adults have the courts at their disposal on equal terms: the adults do not have preferential treatment although, unfortunately, the stronger sometimes obtain priority.

Facilities for running, jumping, etc., are generally easy to fit into a play park, and are certainly of relevance. They can remain unused for long periods, but a fantastic interest will suddenly flare up and they will be in constant use from morning till evening for weeks. Sometimes the children create their own sports clubs within the play park and it then becomes easy to start a very happy and positive programme of competitions between various play parks if leadership encourages it. This can almost amount to small Olympic Games and, of course, adds greatly to the popularity of play parks.

4

3

1 Permanent equipment for table tennis, Stuttgart, W. Germany
2 Permanent tables of 'eternite' on a frame of iron tubes: good shelter from the wind is essential
3 Ball game area in New York, designed by M. Paul Friedberg & Associates
4 Several small ball courts are preferable to one big one

195

Play Apparatus

The words "play apparatus" are themselves dispiriting, but worse still are the mechanical "fairground attractions", having little to do with truly constructive and creative play, that they have often described. Nevertheless, good play apparatus still has its place. For instance, who would wish to do away with the swings or the slides?

Correctly incorporated into the play environment they form a popular and exciting feature which it would be hard to dispense with. It is, however, necessary to bear in mind that play apparatus is subordinate playground furniture, which should be incorporated according to its function, taking safety and the other

aspects of the playground into account. No playground is achieved with play apparatus alone however well thought-out it may be. This is far too often forgotten, and it may well be that this very forgetfulness is the cause of most of our failures.

1 The springy branches of a fallen treè are very popular on a playground
2 Climbing net at Tsukishina, Tokyo
3 Because of its elasticity, a commando's bridge is far better than fixed climbing equipment
4 Horidome, Tokyo

CLIMBING

1

3

2

4

7

8

9

6

10

12

11

13

6 The familiar jungle gym has more play
   potential than one might suppose
7, 8 This kind of equipment should be at the
   highest point of the playground, so that
   the climb is worthwhile
9 Play equipment at Albertslund, Denmark
10 Wooden ladder, Copenhagen
11, 12 Wooden units for play, designed
   by Löfstedt & Quennerstedt
13 Climbing tree, designed by Olof Nola

SLIDES

1 The little girl mounting the ladder could fall backwards; such accidents sometimes happen, and it is better to arrange the slide so that a ladder is not needed
2 A low slide of generous width does not require much courage and can be used in a lot of different ways
3 Bedded in a natural slope, Helsingborg, Sweden
4 Above the rocks at a play park in Gothenburg
5 For a good slide you need a gradient of 1:1 in places to get up to speed
6 If the slope is not steep enough a few steps can be added to increase the gradient, as at this playground at Stuttgart

Photo: Matthews and Evans   1

Photo: Stig Billing   3

200

4

5

6

7

8

Photo: Mary Mitchell

9

7   Slide in sections that can be built up to fit
any slope. Designed by Olof Nola
8   The slide in use in winter
9   The ground can be modelled to meet play
requirements. Nuneaton, England
10   Down the roof at the children's zoo in
Copenhagen
11, 12, 13   Triya-minami, Tokyo
14   Lakewood Park, Sunnivale, California

10

The playground of Iriya minami in Tokyo is dominated by a huge mound of soil dug out during the construction of the underground railway. It is climbed by a path winding up through dense shrub planting, and a flight of steps intersected by the path. Two slides descend from a tubular steel structure on the summit, suspended some 3·5 m (12 ft) above the level of the mound.

11

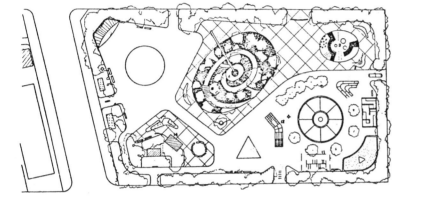

12

13

14

SWINGS

Photo: Bertil Stilling

1

2

3

5

6

4

7

1 The best surface under a swing is a deep
  layer of soft sand, which should extend
  well to the front and rear so that children
  can safely jump from the swing in flight.
  Sea-washed sand is best, and tyre seats
  safest
2 Cradle seat, meant for infants, is still popular
  with older children
3 Infants can manage tyre seats but the cradle
  type is preferable
4 All equipment near the dwelling should be
  of a kind that small children can safely use
  unattended
5 A protective barrier is needed to prevent
  children accidentally running into moving
  swings
6 Swings with fabric seats at a playground in
  Sunnyvale, California
7 With sand beneath the swings, good
  drainage is essential

Play with ropes

Play with ropes has become quite a marked feature of the more recent avant-garde playgrounds in England. It is often of the "Tarzan" variety. You swing by the ropes from tree to tree, or from one platform to another. Its popularity is unbelievable and it attracts young people up to twenty years of age. Such games can be very advanced and naturally not without danger if equipment and method of suspension are not carefully supervised. This type of play can be arranged to offer varying degrees of difficulty, so that even the very young children are catered for. All that is needed is a platform at a suitable level and a rope hung at the right distance and height for a pendular motion to be achieved. The longer the rope the wider the arc and the more advanced the game.

The simplest way of being a Tarzan is to tie a rope around a tree trunk and throw the loose end over a convenient branch so that it can be reached from the ground, but even here some kind of platform is needed to launch yourself from.

Still simpler arrangements with cords and ropes have been successfully tried, and the field is wide open for further experimentation.

1   Rope ride fixed between two climbing posts
    at a play park in London
2   Temperaturen play park, Gothenburg
3, 4, 5   Some kind of suitably raised platform
    is important for a good ride. Notting Hill,
    London

1

2

4

3

5

6

10

7

Photo: Nic Nilsson

8

9

6 Design by Olof Nola
7 Paved mound around a sand area for rope
   games. Gothenburg
8 A bridge of two slack ropes is fascinating
   but not at all easy to cross
9 Orrholmen, Karlstad, Sweden
10 With a rope from the top you can swing
   out and round from one side of the tower
   to the other

Rest and quiet play

Photo: Gösta Glase

5

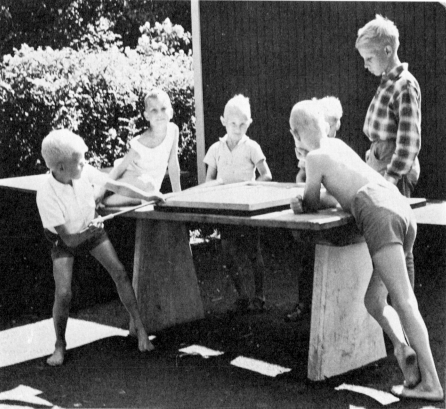

Photo: Stig Billing

4

6

1 Mothers, too, like to sit at a table
2 Every playground needs some sort of
  furniture for work and quiet play
3 Movable chairs and tables have the great
  advantage over fixed ones that you can put
  them just where you want them
4, 5 For carpentry and some games, benches
  fixed to the table would be in the way
6 Play is also observing and just hopefully
  waiting for whatever turns up

211

Old car tyres

Old, worn car tyres are waste material today, and can generally be had for nothing from garages. This source is fully exploited in Gothenburg, since we have found car tyres particularly useful in playgrounds. They are excellent as swing seats and are good moulding tables in the sandpits; indeed there is no limit to their different uses.

The tyres are of course most entertaining when used as loose material that can be thrown aside after the inspiration of the moment. Unfortunately, it is not always possible to permit such play in a general playground, because the tyres are soon found all over the estate; but even as fixed play equipment they are exceptionally useful. The tyres make building units which can be joined to make almost anything: a well to crawl into, a little cave to hide in. If a stack is laid on the ground it becomes a tunnel, and with the help of a frame of iron or wood there is no limit to what can be achieved. Tyres have a natural elasticity, which it is fun to experiment with.

Shipwrecked
To get as far as possible without touching the ground is an old game which crops up again and again in various guises when the conditions are right. It is best if the child itself can arrange the obstacles with suitable material, but in a public playground this is not always possible. A permanent arrangement is therefore better than nothing, and that is easily provided. In the Bergkristallen playground at Gothenburg, old car tyres in various patterns play a dominant role.

1, 3   Tyres have a natural elasticity which makes them very useful for many kinds of play equipment
2   Haginaka play park, Tokyo
4, 5, 6   Tyres can be joined to make a well to crawl into, a cave to hide in
7   Very useful under the see-saw

1

2

6

3

4

5

7

A roof to climb on—a roof to crawl under

A roof can have many functions and, in a playground, all will be used if the children have their way. The roof often becomes a favoured place, where many hours can be spent. The elevated space gives a feeling of security : one commands the surroundings, at least visually, and at the same time the area is nicely secluded for daydreamers.

A roof is also something to get under whenever one needs protection against the sun or a sudden shower. It gives a safe and sheltered feeling to have a roof over one's head, and this covered sitting space often becomes the natural meeting place within an area : during the day for children and, often, in the evening for young people. The latter group has at least an equal need for some kind of fixed place to meet in out-of-doors. The greatest problem attached to the common use of an area in this way is the tidying up that is necessary every morning, particularly the problem of cigarette ends, which can directly endanger the life of small children.

Winter play

Where does a child play during the winter? After all, it is not as if even we, living in the north, have nothing but snowbound winters when the whole town can serve as a playground. Not everybody has natural skating ponds or hills for tobogganing at their disposal, but one would almost think so, looking at the playgrounds in our towns and listening to the debate that goes on. Playgrounds often cease to function at the end of the summer. The playthings are put away and the playground personnel—if they exist—are transferred to other employment, etc.

Admittedly winter is a difficult time in which to make provisions for play, especially when there is neither snow nor ice, and it is cold, wet and unpleasant in every way. From the children's point of view these periods are also the worst. During such times playgrounds are needed more than ever, but they must be appropriate for winter as well, and provide all the diversions possible, however limited. This is the time for cheerfulness and initiative, and it is certainly then that play personnel are needed, much more than in summer. Playthings should not be stored away in winter except for reasons of safety. Leave the swings out, by all means! They are needed far more than during the summer as there is little else to keep busy with. The same applies to the slides. Increase the number of push-carts of different kinds, or anything that is useful for stimulating the children and keeping them on the move.

But most important of all is a heated playroom which gives a choice of play in and out of doors. Neither children nor personnel enjoy being outside for long periods when it is cold and wet.

1

2

216

5

3

6

4

1, 3, 6   Wooden play equipment has the great
advantage of not being too cold to the
touch in winter. Design by Olof Nola
2   Winter play must be considered when
planning a playground
4   Leave the swings out during winter !
5   A few buckets of water can work wonders

217

Winter playground in a tent, Västerås, Sweden

Design: Palle Nielsen

The project was carried out in co-operation with the town of Västerås and the HSB building society. The tent, which has an area of 600 sq. m (720 sq. yd), was hired and positioned centrally within the Råby housing estate. The intention was to provide a heated playground for different ages during the winter months. The playground within the tent (named "the balloon") has some of the character of an adventure playground, with certain fixed equipment such as slides, a climbing frame, sand pits, working benches, café, etc. The following extract from the playground's programme, which was distributed within the estate, gives an idea of the activities carried out in it and of the aim of the project :

"You can slide on the slides. Many of you can slide at the same time. You can sit at the table and drink coffee. There is coffee in the slot machine. You can dress up so that you become a little more beautiful, or funnier or uglier. You can climb up the slide, the climbing frame or the climbing platform. You can also hang on the ropes that run from the climbing frame to the slide. You can swing, several at a time, on the communal swing. The slide is also a communal

1

slide. You can paint. You can paint what you wish in the balloon. Between times you can watch a performance on the stage. Or you can act yourself. The stage is also a dance floor. You can put on the tape recorder. To dance, you only need to move to the music. You can climb the climbing frame and jump down into the plastic foam. If you wish to paint

little pictures, you can sit at the little table. You can use the tools and make something for yourself or something you wish to remain in the balloon. You can build with sand in the sand pit. It is warm inside. You can build and do carpentry, as there are plenty of the boards, planks, sticks, nails and so on that you will need."

Photo: Gullers AB

2

Photo: Gullers AB

4

3

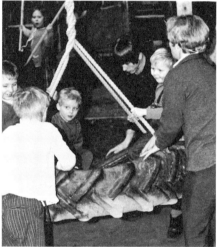

5

1 Painting, coffee-drinking or whatever you want
2 How it looks from outside
3 Carpentry corner
4 Jumping from the climbing structure into foam rubber
5 Roundabout and swing from an old tractor tyre

219

Even adults need to play

If children are poorly provided with outdoor amenities in our modern towns, the same is true for adults—in spite of all the green grass areas. The questions to be asked are these : how much pleasure does this splendid outdoors give, and how much is available for use anyway ? Where are the park benches and chairs, and the tables to gather round ? Sometimes one can wander for miles in the green areas of new housing developments for 10,000 or so people without finding so much as a bench to sit on. Why is there this parsimony out of doors in an otherwise satisfactory area ? It is not unreasonable to say that the communal green in a housing estate should be a replacement for the individual gardens that, for various reasons, we are forced to do without. Or have we so misunderstood the meaning and idea of a garden that we think we can replace it with something which is only nice to look at ? "Gardens are for people" as the American landscape architect Thomas Church has said. He is right, of course, and the concept of a garden should also include the outdoor environment of our housing estates. Towns are for people, too.

2

1, 2 Chess in super-size is a popular game in many German parks
3 Boccia at Schlossgarten, Stuttgart

1

3

INDEX

Compiled by Dr Muriel Lock, Member of the Society of Indexers